TREE OF TALES

TREE OF TALES
Tolkien, Literature, and Theology

Edited by

Trevor Hart and Ivan Khovacs

BAYLOR UNIVERSITY PRESS

Unless otherwise stated scripture quotations are from the New Revised Standard Version Bible, copyright 1989, Division of Christian Education of the National Council of the Churches of Christ in the United States of America. Used by permission. All rights reserved.

Cover Design by David Alcorn, Alcorn Publication Design

Library of Congress Cataloging-in-Publication Data

Tree of tales : Tolkien, literature, and theology / edited by Trevor Hart and Ivan Khovacs.
    p. cm.
  Includes bibliographical references and index.
  ISBN 978-1-932792-64-5 (pbk. : alk. paper)
  Printed Case ISBN: 978-1-4813-1467-1

  1. Tolkien, J. R. R. (John Ronald Reuel), 1892-1973--Philosophy. 2. Fantasy fiction, English--History and criticism. 3. Theology in literature. I. Hart, Trevor, 1967- II. Khovacs, Ivan, 1968-

  PR6039.O32Z883 2007
  823'.912--dc22
                                                    2007007096

TABLE OF CONTENTS

PREFACE

J. R. R. Tolkien is best known for his achievements as a writer of fantasy, and Peter Jackson's recent adaptation of *The Lord of the Rings* for the screen has rekindled interest in the book and all things associated with it. What is less often remembered or acknowledged, though, is Tolkien's lifelong concern with questions of theory-literary, aesthetic, and (in a proper if not always explicit sense) "theological." From the time of his own earliest ventures of an imaginative or creative sort, he pondered the significance and the value of what he was doing. What did it mean that human beings were capable of such acts of imagination? What role did the relevant outputs (myth, fairy story, fantasy, and others) play in the shaping of human life and cultures? What did any of it have to do with the nature and shape of reality as more widely understood? And, as a committed Christian, he could not help but reflect on how this human capacity for acts of "creativity" should be thought of in relation to God's own unique prerogative as Creator of "all things visible and invisible," as the Nicene Creed has it.

In March 1939 Tolkien paid a visit to the town of St. Andrews and delivered the University's Andrew Lang Lecture on the theme "fairy stories." In the essay duly based on this lecture he grappled with some of these same questions, making what one recent commentator refers to as "a plea for the power of literary art," and in the process tendering some suggestive claims about the centrality of mythopoeic imagination in human existence and articulating the outline of a theologically nuanced understanding of artistry as "sub-creation." This lecture marked a key moment in Tolkien's development. Some of its distinctive themes can already be traced in earlier pieces (the poem "Mythopoiea," for instance, and the 1936 lecture *"Beowulf:* the Monsters and the Critics"), but now he took the opportunity to pull threads together and clarify his thinking further. And, as he himself was later to recognize, the ideas articulated here both furnished the immediate personal warrant and the theoretical underpinning for pressing on with the massive literary work upon which he had already, but as yet tentatively, embarked, and which would take him another decade to complete.

On 8 March 2004, the Institute for Theology, Imagination and the Arts in the University of St. Andrews hosted a symposium to mark the 65th anniversary of Tolkien's Andrew Lang Lecture. Papers were read, taking Tolkien's ideas and publications as their focus; there was a panel discussion and an exhibition mounted by the university library's Department of Special Collections; the day culminated with another Andrew Lang Lecture, delivered by Professor David Lyle Jeffrey of Baylor University and engaging with themes that, since Tolkien raised them in 1939, have become more rather than less relevant and urgent.

The present volume draws together and supplements the proceedings of that commemorative occasion. Its contents approach Tolkien's work deliberately from various different disciplinary perspectives, though the boundaries between these are not always easy (or helpful) to draw too precisely. The result, we believe, captures something of the multi-faceted nature of Tolkien's own distinctive concerns and contribution.

Thanks are due to all those who participated in the symposium, especially those who wrote (and have reworked) papers for inclusion in this volume, and to the University of St. Andrews for inviting David Lyle Jeffrey to deliver an Andrew Lang Lecture to mark the occasion. We are also grateful to the estate of the late Professor Tolkien for granting permission to reproduce in facsimile his hitherto unpublished 1947 letter to Principal T. M. Knox. This letter was kindly made available for reproduction by Dr. Norman H. Reid, keeper of manuscripts and head of the Department of Special Collections, University of St. Andrews Library. Grateful acknowledgment is made to Houghton Mifflin Company and HarperCollins Publishers for permission to quote from various of Tolkien's writings (see separate acknowledgments page for details). The editors have made all reasonable efforts to determine any existing copyright on the image of Fáfnir reproduced on page 10, and would welcome further information.

Trevor Hart
Ivan Khovacs
June 2006

ACKNOWLEDGMENTS

The Letters of J. R. R. Tolkien
— Excerpts from *The Letters of J. R. R. Tolkien*, edited by Humphrey Carpenter with the assistance of Christopher Tolkien. Copyright © 1981 by George Allen & Unwin, Publishers, Ltd. eprinted by permission of Houghton Mifflin Company. All rights reserved.
— Excerpts from *The Letters of J. R. R. Tolkien* reprinted by permission of HarperCollins Publishers Ltd. Copyright © J. R. R. Tolkien, 1981.

The Lord of the Rings
— Excerpts from *The Lord of the Rings* by J. R. R. Tolkien. Copyright © 1954, 1955, 1965, 1966 by J. R. R. Tolkien. Copyright © Renewed 1982, 1983 by Christopher R. Tolkien, Michael H. R. Tolkien, John F. R. Tolkien, and Priscilla M. A. R. Tolkien. Reprinted by permission of Houghton Mifflin Company. All rights reserved.
— Excerpts from *The Lord of the Rings* by J. R. R. Tolkien reprinted by permission of HarperCollins Publishers Ltd. Copyright © J. R. R. Tolkien, 1954.

Tree and Leaf
— Excerpts from *Tree and Leaf* by J. R. R. Tolkien. Copyright © 1964 by George Allen & Unwin Ltd. Copyright © Renewed 1992 by

Chapter 1

TOLKIEN, ST. ANDREWS, AND DRAGONS

Rachel Hart

In a letter to the Houghton Mifflin Company in the summer of 1955, John Ronald Reuel Tolkien stated:

> I think the so-called "fairy-story" one of the highest forms of litera-
> ture, and quite erroneously associated with children (as such). But my
> views on that I set out in a lecture delivered at St. Andrew's [sic] (on
> the Andrew Lang foundation, eventually published in *Essays Presented
> to Charles Williams* by Oxford University Press, as "On Fairy-Stories").
> I think it is quite an important work, at least for anyone who thinks
> me worth considering at all.[1]

"It was intimated that the Andrew Lang Lecture on 'Fairy stories' was delivered by Professor J. R. R. Tolkien, M.A., Rawlinson and Bosworth Professor of Anglo-Saxon in the University of Oxford, in the United College Hall on Wednesday, 8th inst, at 5.30 p.m."[2] So read the minutes of the meeting of the Senatus Academicus of the University of St. Andrews, held on 10 March 1939. Tolkien had originally been one of three prospective Andrew Lang lecturers recommended to the Senatus by the Faculty of Arts of the University in June 1938, the others being Professor Gilbert Murray of Oxford and the Right Honourable Lord

Hugh Macmillan.[3] Letters of invitation were duly issued by the Secretary to the University to Murray and Macmillan in the first instance, but both indicated that they were unable to undertake the lecture due to the number of their engagements. It was on 8 October 1938, therefore, that the University approached Tolkien, requesting that he deliver the Andrew Lang Lecture in the University of St. Andrews on the following terms: "The Lecturer is supposed to deliver at least one Lecture during his tenure of office, the subject to be 'Andrew Lang and his Work' or one or other of the many subjects on which he wrote. The amount of the stipend is small, being only £30."[4] A number of letters were exchanged, at the end of which the University had managed to secure the date of 8 March 1939 for Tolkien to come to St. Andrews.[5]

The Andrew Lang lectureship had been established by Sir Peter Redford Scott Lang, Regius Professor of Mathematics in the University from 1879 to 1921. His will of November 1922 made provision for the founding of a lectureship in memory of Andrew Lang, to be delivered on those terms cited to Tolkien. The will gave examples of those subjects in which Lang had been proficient: "History of Scotland, History of St. Andrew, History and Literature of the Scottish Borders, Homer, Greek Literature, English Literature, Poetry, Ballads, Custom and Myth, Archaeology, Antiquities, Prince Charlie, Witchcraft, Joan of Arc, Natural Religions etc."[6] Scott Lang's tribute to his friendship with Andrew Lang has enabled "the sifted memories and judgments of the man and his work by men to whom he had meant much through most of their own reading or writing lives" in the years since the acceptance of the original endowment of £750 by the University Court in December 1926.[7] Tolkien's choice of "Fairy Stories" as his subject picked up on that aspect of Lang's work which had perhaps been most influential upon him from childhood, as "a reader and lover" of fairy stories but "not a student" of them as Andrew Lang was.[8]

The timing of the request from St. Andrews was fortuitous. Early in 1938 Tolkien was to have read a paper to the Lovelace Society, an undergraduate group at Worcester College, Oxford, on the subject of fairy stories, but the paper was not ready in time and he decided instead to read a then unpublished fantasy story, "Farmer Giles."[9] So the invitation from Scotland provided a second opportunity for Tolkien to reflect on and justify his own world of faërie, then developing from *The Hobbit* into *The Lord of the Rings*, the first chapters of which had already been completed. "He felt strongly that fairy stories are not necessarily for children and he decided to devote much of his lecture to the proof of this belief."[10] In his *Letters*, Tolkien says that he was subject to the "contemporary delusions about 'fairy stories' and children. I had to think about it, however, before I gave an 'Andrew Lang' lecture at St. Andrews on fairy stories; and I must say I think the result was entirely beneficial to *The Lord of the Rings*, which was a practical demonstration of the views that I expressed."[11] The lecture was given at the end of the first third of his literary career and now forms part of "Tolkien's most influential contributions to scholarship and criticism."[12]

Commentators on Tolkien seem to agree with him as to the significance of the Andrew Lang Lecture as a critical analysis of the form to which he was to devote so much of his subsequent labors. Randel Helms states that in his 1936 lecture, "*Beowulf:* The Monsters and the Critics," as well as in his Andrew Lang Lecture: "Tolkien came gradually to terms with the form that had captured him; he described and evaluated it, slowly, carefully preparing himself and an audience for the book *The Hobbit* taught him how to write, the book he had already begun when he delivered the *Beowulf* lecture: *The Lord of the Rings*."[13] William Green cites "On Fairy-Stories" as "important background for reading *The Hobbit*,"[14] as "the resolution of a weighty midlife question," and as evidence that "[Tolkien] is reassuring himself that he has taken the right turn, that he will not be wasting his life if he devotes his best years to expanding the world of *The Hobbit*."[15] Michael White's biography of Tolkien notes: "As well as this lecture being a piece of analysis of a literary form so close to Tolkien's heart, it served to focus his own thoughts about his new work."[16] Brian Rosebury declares the lecture to be "a complex essay in implicit self-analysis and self exhortation from the most fruitful phase of his career."[17] As for the effect of having taken time out to analyze what he was doing, Carpenter says that, after having delivered the lecture, "Tolkien returned with a new enthusiasm to the story whose purpose he had justified. That story had been begun as a mere 'sequel' to *The Hobbit*, at the instigation of his publisher, but now, especially after the declaration of high purpose that he had made in the lecture, the Ring was as important to him as the Silmarils."[18]

Sadly for the University of St. Andrews, in view of its significance, the text of Tolkien's lecture was not secured for publication, as every other Lang Lecture delivered before 1960 had been. Those from 1927/28 to 1937/38 were eventually published as *Concerning Andrew Lang, being the Andrew Lang Lectures delivered before the University of St. Andrews, 1927–1937*, with an introduction by A. Blyth Webster and a preface by J. B. Salmond. There were no Andrew Lang lectures during the Second World War, and so the next lecture after Tolkien's was delivered by Emeritus Professor Gilbert Murray in 1946/47, succeeded by Lord Macmillan of Aberfeldy in the following academic year. Their lectures, and most subsequent ones, have been printed in pamphlet form.[19]

There is a letter in the University of St. Andrews muniment collection that indicates that there had been an agreement with Oxford University Press to print the texts of the first ten lectures, which it had been hoped would have been done in time for the centenary of Lang's birth in 1944. Tolkien's was the eleventh lecture. However, the war intervened and the volume was not finally produced until 1949. It seems likely, in view of Tolkien's reluctance to let his material be published without his extremely careful revision and amendment,[20] that he would have retained his text in order to rework it to his own satisfaction before allowing its publication. The lecture was, of course, first published as "On Fairy-Stories," his contribution to *Essays Presented to Charles Williams*,[21] which predated the University's publication of the first Andrew Lang Lectures by two years.

Further light is cast on the publication of the lecture in a letter from Tolkien, dated 17 December 1947, preserved among the papers of Principal T. Malcolm Knox (1900–1988) within the manuscript collection of the University of St. Andrews Library[22] (see Figure 1). The document appears to be a cover letter for Tolkien's gift to Knox of a copy of the Charles Williams *Essays*, his contribution to which he describes in the most typically self-deprecatory of terms. Wayne Hammond's *J. R. R. Tolkien: A Descriptive Bibliography* gives the date of publication of the *Essays* as December 1947,[23] so it can be assumed that Tolkien is enclosing a copy of the newly published work for Knox. Tolkien refers to his gift as "the

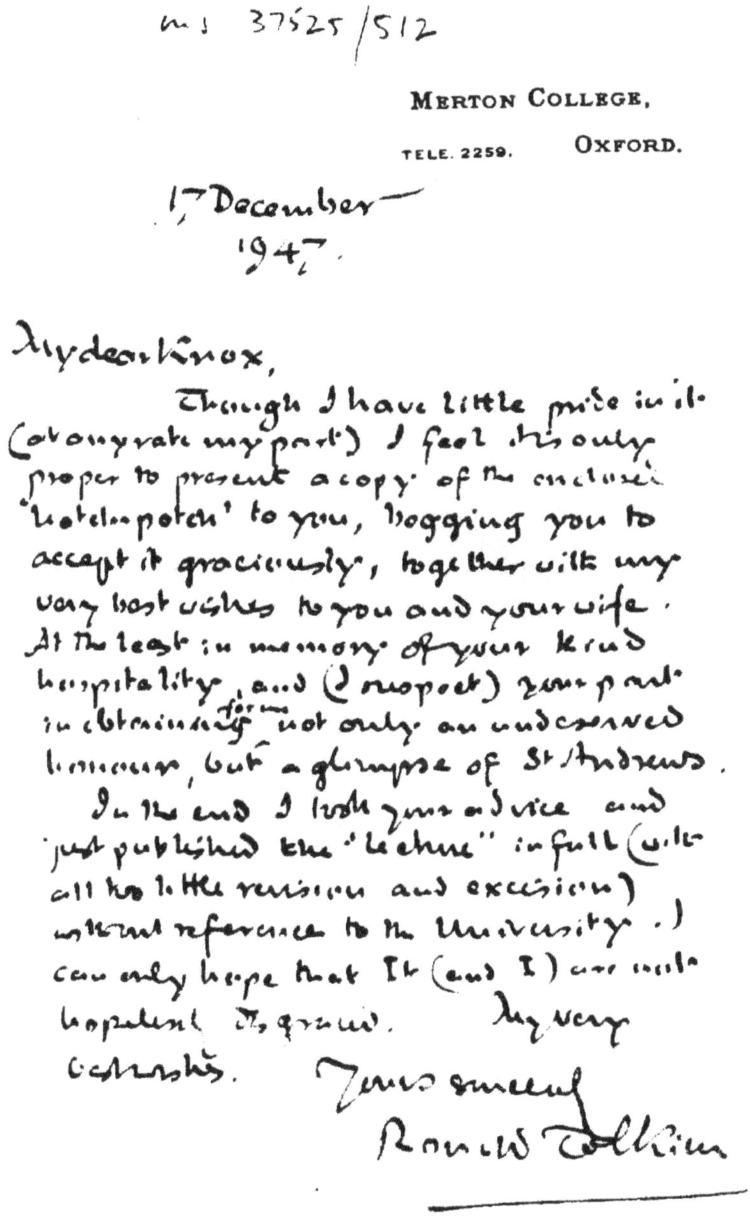

Figure 1: Letter from J.R.R. Tolkien to T. Malcolm Knox, Principal of the University of St. Andrews, 17 December 1947.

enclosed "hotch-potch.'" The very same phrase is used to describe the collection by C. S. Lewis on page v of its preface.

Tolkien's letter implies that he stayed with Professor and Mrs. Knox when he visited St. Andrews in 1939 to deliver the lecture and attributes to Knox his nomination as lecturer. Knox was indeed a member of the Faculty of Arts, which sent nominations to the Senatus in 1938. The two men had Oxford in common. Knox had studied as an undergraduate at Pembroke, returning, after a time in business, to a position as lecturer and fellow at Jesus College and lecturer at Queen's College in Greek philosophy from 1931. Thence he moved to the professorship of moral philosophy in St. Andrews in 1936. Tolkien's appointment as professor of Anglo-Saxon in 1925 included a professorial fellowship at Pembroke, Knox's alma mater. In 1946 Tolkien moved to Merton as Merton Professor of English Language and Literature.

It is interesting to note that the accession record for the University of St. Andrews Library's copy of *Essays* presented to Charles Williams indicates that the book was purchased on 13 February 1948 upon the recommendation of Professor Knox.[24] Knox presumably retained the copy Tolkien had sent, but he considered the volume a worthy addition to the university library and requested that it be added to stock.

In the final paragraph of the letter to Knox, Tolkien discusses the published version of the Andrew Lang Lecture: "In the end I took your advice and just published the "lecture" in full (with all too little revision and excision) without reference to the University. I can only hope that It (and I) are not hopelessly disgraced." Here we see that Tolkien had been in touch with Knox between the delivery of the lecture and its rewriting for publication, although no trace of such correspondence can be found in the Knox papers. A comparison of extracts cited in local press coverage of the lecture with the text published in *Essays Presented to Charles Williams* reveals some verbatim correspondence,[25] confirming Tolkien's claim that he did not completely revise it. That he did not excise much but on the contrary incorporated a fair amount of new material into the published version is also confirmed by the 1947 text, which (apart from its considerable length) makes explicit reference to St. Andrews and to the delivery of the lecture there "in abbreviated form."[26] When Tolkien revised "On Fairy-Stories" for inclusion in *Tree and Leaf* in 1964, he omitted many of the contextual references to St. Andrews. However, his personal connection with the town was rekindled around that time, since in a letter of 1964 he notes that his eldest grandchild is "now at St. Andrews."[27] This was Michael George David Reuel Tolkien, who graduated M.A. with honors of the first class in English language and literature on 1 July 1966.[28]

On 8 March 2004 the Institute for Theology, Imagination and the Arts within the School of Divinity at the University of St. Andrews held a symposium on Tolkien, incorporating an Andrew Lang Lecture by David Jeffrey. The date of this event was chosen to mark the 65th anniversary of the delivery of Tolkien's Andrew Lang Lecture, of which the present volume is the record. In the context of that gathering, an exhibition was arranged of relevant materials from the Special Collections Department of the University of St. Andrews Library. The Library holds the extensive Andrew Lang Collection, from which selected items were put on show,[29] as well as the aforementioned letter from Tolkien to Knox and other related items. The aim was to demonstrate something of the expertise developed by Lang in the study of fairy tales, that aspect of his work which was picked up by Tolkien in his 1939 lecture first entitled simply "Fairy Stories."

The early influence of Andrew Lang's fairy stories[30] on Tolkien is explicitly documented in Tolkien's own writings. He was encouraged to read by his mother, and those story books which appealed included Red Indian stories, the "Curdie" books of George MacDonald, stories of Merlin and Arthur, "but most of all he found delight in the Fairy Books of Andrew Lang, especially the *Red Fairy Book*."[31] In "On Fairy-Stories" he states:

> [T]he Fairy Story Books of Lang are not, perhaps, lumber rooms. They are more like stalls in a rummage-sale. Someone with a duster and a fair eye for things that retain some value has been round the attics and box-rooms. His collections are largely a by-product of his adult study of mythology and folk-lore, but they were made into and presented as books for children. . . . Now I was one of the children whom Andrew Lang was addressing. I was born at about the same time as the *Green Fairy Book*.[32]

But it was the *Red Fairy Book* which was Tolkien's favorite, "for tucked away in its closing pages was the best story he had ever read. This was the tale of Sigurd who slew the dragon Fáfnir" from "The Volsunga Saga."[33] Tolkien wrote, in "On Fairy-Stories," of Fáfnir, "the prince of all dragons . . . [t]he dragon had the trade-mark *Of Faërie* written plain upon him. In whatever world he had his being it was an Other-world. Fantasy, the making or glimpsing of Other-worlds, was the heart of the desire of Faërie. I desired dragons with a profound desire."[34]

There are five drawings to illustrate "The story of Sigurd" in the *Red Fairy Book*, the first of which, on page 359, shows Fáfnir the dragon. A copy of the 1890 edition of Lang's *Red Fairy Book* from the Andrew Lang Collection was put on display in St. Andrews in March 2004. The illustrations in the book are by Henry Justice Ford and Lancelot Speed. It is unclear whether Ford or Speed was responsible for the image of Fáfnir, since there appears to be no signature on the illustration, but the other four drawings for this story are clearly signed "L. Speed." A careful examination of the rest of the volume indicates that one of the illustrators was responsible for all the pictures in each complete story. Therefore, by implication, the drawing of Fáfnir is by Speed. The style is, however, admittedly more like Ford's. Ford "mixed carefully observed objects from the real world with fantasy creatures from an imagined world in a very convincing way. His penwork is assured and clear. . . . A whole generation of Edwardians grew up on Ford's illustrations to Andrew Lang's fairy tales, the long series of little books appearing between 1889 and 1913."[35]

The 1890 *Red Fairy Book* image of Fáfnir shows a horned and whiskered dragon with prominent ears, with wisps of smoke curling from his mouth; long, scaly, and lizard-like, in the act of emerging through a hole in a wall, descending to the floor of his cave, which is littered with human skulls and bones. His front legs are visible, the right one clearly showing claws.[36]

Tolkien represented dragons, those creatures to him so evocative of faërie, in both words and pictures. In their magnificent *J. R. R. Tolkien: Artist and Illustrator*, Wayne G. Hammond and Christina Scull provide an excellent analysis of Tolkien's dragons,[37] building on Scull's earlier work. This appeared as "Dragons from Andrew Lang's Retelling of

Sigurd to Tolkien's Chrysophylax" in *Leaves from the Tree: J. R. R. Tolkien's Shorter Fiction*.[38] She identifies a chronology of dragons: from Tolkien, age 7, reflecting on his "great green dragon"[39] (49); through Glorund/Glaurung in *The Book of Lost Tales*, part II, written about 1919, published in 1984, as "the most powerful, malicious and totally evil of Tolkien's dragons" (50); the dragons of "The Fall of Gondolin"; then the dragon in the poem "The Hoard," published in *The Gryphon* (50), who is very similar to Smaug in *The Hobbit* (51); then Chrysophylax in *Farmer Giles of Ham* (51–52); followed by Glomund in "The Later Annals of Beleriand," written in the 1930s (52); and finally "The Dragon's Visit," published in 1937 and 1965 (53). In the second half of her paper she analyzes the treatment of dragons by Tolkien's contemporaries. Hammond and Scull together also include his illustrations of dragons, coiled, flying, and fighting knights. However, perhaps Tolkien's most well-known visual representation of a dragon remains Smaug in *The Hobbit*.

On 1 January 1938, Tolkien delivered a Christmas lecture to children on the subject of dragons at the Oxford University Museum. He discerned two sorts of dragons, "'creeping' and 'winged'" but, in general, large, deadly, coiling serpent-creatures."[40] He showed a slide of the last of his *Hobbit* watercolors to illustrate *draco fabulosus*, "a serpent creature . . . 20 feet or more."[41] Smaug does not have quite the majesty of Glorund but is every bit as dangerous and just as capable of creating a desolation. The original impression of *The Hobbit* in 1937 had contained no colored pictures, but the second English impression of the same year and the first American edition in 1938 included five colored pictures by Tolkien,[42] one of which was entitled "O Smaug, the Chiefest and Greatest of Calamities," Bilbo Baggins's words to the dragon in chapter 12—an illustration now more familiarly known as *Conversation with Smaug* and completed by Tolkien in July 1937.[43] In this familiar picture we see the dragon lying on his heap of treasure, with his belly toward the top of the pile, so that he is lying curled downwards, with his head resting on the hoard, smoke issuing from his nostrils and his ears pointed and alert, his right clawed foot extended. Littering the floor of the cave are human skulls and bones.

Hammond and Scull have already established that Tolkien's own visualization of scenes was often heavily influenced by earlier pictures with which he was familiar. Thus, as Brian Alderson notes in *The Hobbit, 50th Anniversary*, the basic composition of "The Trolls" in *The Hobbit* is borrowed from an illustration for *Hansel and Grethel* by Jennie Harbour in a book of fairy tales (*The Fairy Tale Book* by Edric Vredenburg). Also, the eagle in Tolkien's "Bilbo Woke Up with Early Sun in His Eyes" is adapted from Alexander Thorburn's "Golden Eagle (Immature)" in Lord Lilford's *Birds of the British Islands* (1891). Finally, Professor J. S. Ryan in "Two Oxford Scholars' Perceptions of the Traditional Germanic Hall"[44] highlighted Tolkien's use of E. V. Gordon's "Interior of a Norse Hall" as the model for *Firelight in Beorn's House*.[45] No one, though, seems yet to

Figure 2: Fáfnir the dragon, from "The Story of Sigurd" in Andrew Lang, Red Fairy Book (London: Longman, Green, 1890), 359.

have identified the likely source for one of Tolkien's most distinctive and familiar depictions, a link suggested by the juxtaposition of two images (Tolkien's aforementioned *Conversation with Smaug* and the drawing of Fáfnir from the *Red Fairy Book* of Andrew Lang [see Figure 2]) in the exhibition mounted in St. Andrews in March 2004.[46]

Careful consideration of the two drawings reveals clear compositional similarities in the shape and alignment of the dragon's shoulder, neck, and forearms—particularly the right claw—the skulls scattered on the floor, and the wisps of smoke arising from the head. The basic configuration of the dragon in the *Red Fairy Book* illustration clearly remained with Tolkien (whether or not we must suppose him to have had it in front of him) when, in 1937, he duly came to commit this particular "dragon" form, Smaug, to paper.[47] Perhaps the clinching piece of evidence, however, is in what Tolkien himself referred to as his "low philological jest"[48]—the choice of the name for his dragon. Originally the dragon in *The Hobbit* was called "Pryftan" but Tolkien changed its name to Smaug. Various interpretations have been offered for the name: *smog* meaning "brimstone, smoke and vapor of a dragon"; the Old English influences of *smeagan* meaning to "inquire into"; *smeagol* meaning "burrowing, working into"; and Tolkien's preferred *smugan*, from the past tense of the primitive Germanic verb *Smugan*, "to squeeze through a hole."[49] The *Red Fairy Book* has a dragon squeezing through a hole in a wall, down onto the cave floor which is littered with skulls and bone.

It seems appropriate to conclude with Carpenter's quotation from Tolkien and his comments on it:

> "One writes such a story," said Tolkien, "out of the leaf-mould of the mind"; . . . One learns little by raking through a compost heap to see what dead plants originally went into it. Far better to observe its effect on the new and growing plants that it is enriching. And in *The Hobbit*, the leaf-mould of Tolkien's mind nurtured a rich growth with which only a few other books in children's literature can compare.[50]

Chapter 2

THE FAIRY STORY: J. R. R. TOLKIEN
AND C. S. LEWIS

Colin Duriez

INTRODUCTION

Imagine a world in which there was no *The Chronicles of Narnia* or *The Lord of the Rings*, *Mere Christianity* or Aragorn, Lucy, or Galadriel. It is likely that, but for J. R. R. Tolkien, you would never have read C. S. Lewis. It is just as likely that, without C. S. Lewis, you would not have enjoyed Tolkien's work.

In this chapter I shall first give a brief overview of the friendship of Tolkien and C. S. Lewis to indicate the importance of their friendship and mutuality. I shall then try to focus upon their preoccupation with rehabilitating fantasy and fairy story, with learning and education in contrast to training, and with a recovery of insights into reality and the values of what Lewis called the Old West—insights and values they considered of supreme importance. In this focusing, I shall refer briefly to some of their writings in the golden years of their friendship—particularly from the late 1920s to the outbreak of the World War II. This will include a glance at Lewis's publication in 1939 of a collection called *Rehabilitations*, embodying ideas very much shaped in the context of his friendship with Tolkien. In this brief paper, I shall touch on probably the most important works—*The Lord of the Rings* and *The Chronicles of Narnia*—as rehabilitation in practice.

A BRIEF SKETCH OF THEIR MUTUALITY

The two friends enormously influenced each other, but in very different ways. This mutual shaping took place against the backdrop of nearly forty years of friendship, a friendship that had its ups and downs, fun and deep tensions, which reflected differences of temperament, of church-manship, and even of their views of their art. The affinities between the two, however, always outweighed the differences.

Tolkien and Lewis first met at a meeting of Oxford University English School faculty, convened at Merton College on March 11, 1926. Lewis had been a tutor and lecturer in English for nearly an academic year. Tolkien, for the same period, had held the Chair of Anglo-Saxon; a little older than Lewis, he had returned to Oxford after a stint as reader, then professor, of English language at Leeds University.

Tolkien was slight of build, compared with the thickset and taller Lewis, and, in Lewis's view, rather opinionated. In his diary that night Lewis noted: "Nor harm in him: only needs a smack or so." At that time Lewis was an aspiring poet, soon to publish his second book of verse, *Dymer* (1926). Tolkien was a scholar, a philologist, working on obscure papers about Early English literature and language, encourag-ing colleagues to learn Old Icelandic, and rumored to have a private hobby of inventing languages. He was a Roman Catholic with a deep emotional attachment to his faith, connected to the early death of his talented mother. Lewis was at that time still an atheist, committed to a materialist explanation of life and of the origins of human language, though there were some chinks in his armor, which Tolkien began to notice as the friendship developed.

The philologist was soon sharing with Lewis his private construc-tion of the early ages of his invented world—Middle-earth—made up of saga, its own mythology, and developing stories, often in both poetic and prose versions. Lewis was enraptured, as he never failed to be by myth and stories of "romance"—that is, tales that contained glimpses of other worlds. Tolkien also showed Lewis his beautiful but incomplete poetic translation of *Beowulf*.

Tolkien began trying to convince his friend of the truth of Christian faith, culminating in a long night conversation in September 1931. Aided and abetted by H. V. D. "Hugo" Dyson, he argued for the fact that that the gospels have a satisfying imaginative as well as intellectual appeal, demanding a response from the whole person. He more or less accused Lewis of an imaginative failure in not accepting their reality. A few days later Lewis capitulated, and became a Christian believer. The rest is history—well over 100 million sales of *The Lord of the Rings*, perhaps 60 million of the *Narnia* stories, eleven Oscars for a movie retelling of Tolkien's epic romance, and innumerable people who have been touched, the whispers of transcendence made audible for them.

Lewis, therefore, owed an enormous debt to Tolkien. After his conversion he gradually emerged as the unique and perhaps unparalleled Christian communicator we know—writing fiction full of enduring images of God, our humanity, and reality transfigured by the light of heaven, and imaginative prose that has persuaded numerous people throughout the world of the truth of the Christian claims. His basic apologetic strategy was born in those persistent arguments of Tolkien in which imagination and reason are reconciled, and storytelling is at the crux.

Tolkien, in return, also owed a gigantic debt to his friend. Without Lewis's encouragement, he confessed, he would never have completed *The Lord of the Rings*, a huge, meticulous task that took over eleven years. Even before then, *The Hobbit*, the "prequel" to that heroic romance, had initially been known only to his children and to the warmly enthusiastic Lewis.

Writing *The Lord of the Rings* was not simply the forging of a story that has won millions of readers throughout the world. It also marked the creation, or rather rehabilitation, of an adult readership for symbolic stories, and establishing a climate that allowed the making of the recent blockbuster movies. The early years of the Tolkien-Lewis friendship marked a period in which fantasy and fairy tale had been relegated to children's literature. Tolkien effectively enlisted Lewis in the task of rehabilitating these kinds of stories, once enjoyed by warriors in the mead halls and tough enough to be a vehicle for exploring modern questions of global warfare, human evil on an unprecedented scale, and the domination of the machine. This last problem was the subject of Lewis's inaugural lecture when he moved to Cambridge in 1954 to take up the newly created chair of Medieval and Renaissance Literature.

Lewis had clashed with the ethos of the Cambridge English School many times, as in *The Personal Heresy* (coauthored with the Cambridge scholar E. M. W. Tillyard),[1] which attacked the psychologizing of literary works. When the unexpected invitation to the chair came, Lewis turned it down, not once, but twice (partly out of concern over leaving his alcoholic brother, Warren). As persuasive as ever, Tolkien (one of the eight electors for the chair) argued Lewis into accepting. In his colorful inaugural lecture, Lewis expounded a theme central to their friendship and affinity: that the rise of modernism, sociologically expressed in the creation of "the Age of the Machine," was an unprecedented discontinuity in Western civilization.

Tolkien, like his friend, sought to rehabilitate the "Old Western" values the new professor lauded. Against this major affinity, their differences could not break the friendship, despite its cooling in later years, especially after Lewis's relationship with divorcée Joy Davidman.

There were, first of all, theological differences. Lewis was an Anglican, but in an old Puritan tradition of the two Johns, Milton and Bunyan. Tolkien was a pre-Vatican II Roman Catholic, opposed to divorce and remarriage. He also strongly disapproved of Lewis as a popular communicator of the Christian faith—he felt that that task should be the concern of professional theologians. Secondly, there were differences of temperament. Tolkien was a perfectionist, meticulously working and reworking his writing. Lewis, in contrast, seemed to dash off his books—*The Pilgrim's Regress* in a fortnight, the seven *Chronicles of Narnia* in as many years. Thirdly, the two friends differed artistically. Tolkien was the master of the allusive story, relying on his deep faith in a natural theology of the imagination, in which the insights incarnate in the tale would be a vehicle of God's grace to the reader. Lewis was the apologist and evangelist, building-in allegorical signposts that Tolkien artistically disliked. Yet Lewis's last completed fiction—*Till We Have Faces*—in its pagan, pre-Christian setting has a remarkable affinity with Tolkien's art. Ironically, it was composed during the period under which their friendship had cooled, and written under the influence of Joy Davidman, who was an accomplished novelist!

THEIR WRITINGS DURING THIS PERIOD

When the two men met in 1926, Tolkien was a number of years into his construction of an invented mythology and imagined history that came to be called *The Silmarillion*. The posthumously published version of 1977 is a summary construction of the intended work, which is unfinished, complex, vast and multifaceted, and in parts poetic in form. In 1926 it was, as far as Tolkien was concerned, a private hobby. However, he began to share it with C. S. Lewis, which started the process by which it eventually became public. The publication of his children's fairy story, *The Hobbit*, in 1937, was but a stage in the process. The public, of course, had to wait until 1954 and 1955 for the publication in three volumes of *The Lord of the Rings*, the events of which concerned a very brief period in the third age of Tolkien's invented world of Middle-earth.

Soon after Lewis became a Christian believer, Tolkien set down the basic arguments he had employed against his friend's materialism in the poem "Mythopoeia," which, among many things, includes a beatitude to makers of fantasy and legend.[2] These storytellers, writes Tolkien, are blessed as they speak of things outside of recorded time; though they have looked at death and even ultimate defeat, they have not flinched and retreated in despair. Instead, they have often sung of victory, and the fire in their voices, caught from legend, has kindled the hearts of their listeners. In so doing, they have lit up the darkness of both the past and the present day with the brightness of suns "as yet by no man seen." Tolkien also writes of the human heart not being composed of false-hood, but having nourishment of knowledge from the Wise One and still remembering him. For Tolkien, though the estrangement is ancient, human beings are neither completely abandoned by God nor totally corrupted. Though we are disgraced, we still retain vestiges of our mandate to rule; we continue to create according to the "law in which we're made." The poem anticipates his later Andrew Lang Lecture "On Fairy-Stories."

Within a short time Lewis composed his first complete fiction—a tale, like his friend's *The Hobbit*, of there and back again, a motif of fairy story. It was called *The Pilgrim's Regress*, after Bunyan. As an allegory in the mode of his fellow Puritan, *The Pilgrim's Regress* is not a fairy story, but it has some elements of Faërie, such as an invented world. It is, however, Christian fantasy, which has a long and varied history. It is defined by Colin Manlove in his book *Christian Fantasy* as "a fiction dealing with the Christian supernatural, often in an imaginary world."[3] It draws upon the imaginative richness of the Bible, with its integrated and organic picture of both the seen and the unseen world. There are visions in scripture of heaven and God, fantastic beasts and dragons; in realistic settings there is also a talking snake and ass. Its history, the origins of which are perhaps the Arthurian stories of the Middle Ages, includes Dante's fourteenth-century *The Divine Comedy*, the poignant Middle English poem *Pearl*, Spenser's *The Faerie Queene*, Marlowe's *Dr. Faustus*, Bunyan's *The Pilgrim's Progress*, and George MacDonald's *Phantastes* and *Lilith*. *The Pilgrim's Regress* paralleled Lewis's long gestation of medieval allegory, *The Allegory of Love*, in the preface of which he acknowledges Tolkien and other friends—particularly Owen Barfield, a deeply important influence on both Lewis and Tolkien.

In 1936, the year of the publication of *The Allegory of Love*, Tolkien gave a British Academy lecture on *Beowulf*, the Early English poem that so inspired his fiction. This lecture complements the Andrew Lang Lecture of 1939 which set out some of the sacramental significance of fantasy and fairy tale as an appropriate medium of Christian meaning, intimately connected to the mysteries of human language and mind.

In 1938 Lewis published his second work of Christian fantasy (approved, like the first, by Tolkien), this time in the science-fiction genre. *Out of the Silent Planet* was self-consciously part of the strategy of the two men to rehabilitate the fairy story, including the enormous task of restoring it as a medium for grown-ups. Two years earlier, Lewis had tossed a coin after a conversation with Tolkien that determined that he would write a tale of space travel while Tolkien composed one on time travel. (As Tolkien points out in "On Fairy-Stories," exploration of both time and space are important elements in the fairy tale.) After abandoning a story he attempted on time travel "The Lost Road," Tolkien turned his attention to his sequel to *The Hobbit*, which nonetheless, I am convinced, became his successful story of time exploration.

"The Lost Road" highlights Tolkien's preoccupation with the ancient past of Europe, the foreground of which was the Worcestershire and

Warwickshire of his childhood. In the story, Alboin, as he gets older (and pretty much to the age of Tolkien as he wrote "The Lost Road"), reflects on his own life and identifies a persistent longing that has accompanied him since childhood years: a "desire to go back," to revisit not his own past but ancient times, places, and kingdoms, to meet and walk with their inhabitants, and to hear spoken tongues long-since forgotten. Alboin's longings are fulfilled in the sequel to *The Hobbit*. Is not *The Lord of the Rings* Tolkien's enduring story of "time travel," his unrivaled exploration of the nature of time? While there is no obvious device of time-traveling into the past, he was able to create, by a hugely imaginative anachronism, the illusion of Middle-earth as part of the history and background of northern Europe. Though an imagined history, there is a sense of familiarity, in which this ancient and seemingly discovered history can be appropriated by the reader of today, as any history is appropriated. We travel in time as we enjoy the story.

Let us not be hasty, says Treebeard, in *The Lord of the Rings*. However, I must rush to finish my hasty visit to the formative and momentous years of the Tolkien-Lewis friendship with Lewis's collection of essays, *Rehabilitations*. The concerns and affinities of the two friends come out, I believe, in what Lewis calls "a certain unity" in various "beliefs about life and books which are implicit throughout."

REHABILITATIONS

In his brief preface, Lewis states that much of his book praises what he loves, but which is under attack. Six of the nine essays are provoked by these attacks. Two, he points out, "defend great romantic poets against popular hatred or neglect of Romanticism." (Later in the book he observes that romanticism is an ancient feature of literature in English, going back to early medieval times.) Two other essays defend "the present course of English studies at Oxford" (based on a syllabus set up by Tolkien, with Lewis's help, which emphasized humane learning, where undergraduates were considered the fellows of older scholars). A fifth essay "is partly a defense of the many popular books which have, I believe, so greatly increased my power of enjoying more serious literature as well as "real life"; but it is much more a defense of disinterested literary enjoyment against certain other dangerous tendencies in modern education." A further essay champions the study of alliterative verse so brilliantly and natively a feature of Early English poetry—a genre he later on mentions as being employed by Tolkien. Thinking probably of his friend's poetic and unfinished version of the story of Túrin Turambar, from the "matter" of Middle-earth, Lewis writes: "Professor Tolkien will soon, I hope, be ready to publish an alliterative poem." One essay in the collection, "Bluspels and Flalansferes," draws heavily upon the insights of Owen Barfield's *Poetic Diction* (1928), a book to which Tolkien was also greatly indebted.[5] The essay contains some remarkable affinities with two very different Christian thinkers, Herman Dooyeweerd and Michael Polanyi, in focusing upon reality in terms of meaning rather than concept. Lewis champions the imagination as the organ of meaning, involved in all human knowledge of reality; for him the imagination provides a sensing, perceiving, feeling knowledge that is objective but personal. A human facility with metaphor is a condition of winning knowledge. Typically, Lewis states: "a man who says *heaven* and thinks of the visible sky is pretty sure to mean more than a man who tells us that heaven is a state of mind." Provocatively, Lewis tops off the book by discussing the relationship between Christianity and literature, reveling in the importance of unoriginality in premodern times.

The vision underlying the essays in *Rehabilitations*, and indeed all of the writings of Lewis and Tolkien in this period, involves restoration in three main areas:

1. The fairy story and fantasy;
2. "Learning" and education against a modernist overemphasis on "training";
3. Reintroducing values of the "Old West" such as sacrifice, chivalry, hierarchy, freedom, goodness, dignity, beauty, wonder, holiness, friendship, and fellowship.

THE FAIRY STORY AND FANTASY

What was it about fairy stories that led these two men to want to rehabilitate them for a modern audience—adults as well as children? They had both personal and professional reasons for this interest. Personally, as they were growing up, they had both read and enjoyed such stories, in collections by the brothers Grimm, Andrew Lang, and others. Lewis had also heard Celtic myths—his nurse had told him some of the folk tales of Ireland. Professionally, they studied and taught the literatures of medieval romance and, in Tolkien's case, the background of Norse myth. And they realized that it was only quite recently that such stories had become marginalized as "children's stories." Through much of history these were tales told and enjoyed by grown-ups. Even strong warriors enjoyed them, rejoicing in their triumphant moments, weeping at tragic turns of events. These stories told them important things about reality—about who they were and what the world was like, and about the realm of the divine.

It dawned on both men that there was a need to create a readership again for these books—especially an adult readership. Lewis's space trilogy came out of this same impulse to write the sort of stories that he and Tolkien liked to read. He felt he could say things in science fiction that he couldn't say in other ways. Tolkien had been expressing this sentiment already for years when the two men met; ever since World War I, he had been writing hundreds of pages of a cycle of myth and legend from the early ages of Middle-earth.

"LEARNING" AND EDUCATION AGAINST A MODERNIST OVEREMPHASIS ON "TRAINING"

In *Rehabilitations*, Lewis has strong words to say about the importance of humane learning:

> If education is beaten by training, civilization dies. . . . If you press to know what I mean by civilization, I reply "Humanity," by which I do not mean kindness so much as the realization of the human idea. Human life means to me the life of beings for whom the leisured activities of thought, art, literature, conversation are the end, and the preservation and propagation of life merely the means. That is why education seems to me so important: it actualizes that potentiality for leisure, if you like for amateurishness, which is man's prerogative.[6]

He goes on to argue that learning is the realized stage of education. It is an activity for people who have already been humanized by the educative process. Learning is marked by a desire to know; it is intentionally aimed at knowledge as a transcendental good in itself.

REINTRODUCING VALUES OF THE "OLD WEST"

In Narnia, young evacuees from a modern European war encounter a faun, a dwarf, a Snow Queen who is not even of that world, centaurs, a big bad wolf, talking beavers, a giant, dryads, naiads, a unicorn, a huge lion who made the land, and even Father Christmas, complete with gifts. *The Chronicles of Narnia* have as their background an older world that is not dominated by machines and modern weapons. In Lewis's view, this is in fact a vast period, from classical times, through the rise of Christianity and the Christianization of the West, up to early in the nineteenth century. The *Chronicles* in particular draw inspiration from the Middle Ages and the Renaissance, most especially the sixteenth century. This is why Narnia is inhabited by imagined creatures from throughout this vast period—from Roman Bacchus to European Father Christmas. Classical naiads and dryads mix with chivalrous talking mice.

Lewis believed that we live in a world that is fractured from this older world by what he called in his inaugural lecture at Cambridge "a Great Divide," which ushered in the Age of the Machine. Our new age is dominated by a persistent idea of progress in which the past is superseded. The newer (even if it is a new moral attitude) is automatically, no question, superior to the older. By a singular inversion, we now place God in the dock and find him wanting, instead of seeing ourselves as under God's judgment.

Lewis's approach was eclectic (a characteristic of an older poet he loved, Edmund Spenser); he drew freely and widely on the images and stories of the whole of the "Old West." His fellow strategist, Tolkien, had interests that were more focused on the Early English period of literature and northern mythology, but his aims were similar—to encourage contemporary people to appropriate this important older history for themselves, taking it into their contemporary lives instead of simply absorbing the narrow myths and presuppositions of modernism. Tolkien and Lewis wished to open a door that would awaken desires and allow the experience of sensations yet unknown, pointing to a reality beyond "the walls of the world."

The Lord of the Rings embodies the same virtues and values as Lewis's, drawn from this older world, and properly rooted, as he saw it, in the gospel. Providence, sacrifice, meekness, fellowship, and courage against the darkness are just some of the themes that are integral to his story, in which unimagined joy comes after grim ordeal. Behind all events—and perhaps Tolkien's most fundamental theme—is a cosmic battle between good and evil, a theme also deeply embedded in Lewis's writings. This conflict was not conceived in a Manichean way; though evil is a formidable foe and one day the universe will be rid of it.[7] The central event that changed the cosmos, Christ's heroic sacrifice, can only be anticipated in *The Lord of the Rings* (unlike *The Chronicles of Narnia*) as the events of that story are set deep in the pre-Christian era of an imagined northern Europe.

Lewis was inspired by the literature, particularly the stories, of the long-ago world of the West. He hoped that a love for his Narnian tales would encourage a recognition and exploration of the books, stories, and attitudes of this older world which, he felt embodied a remarkably consistent wisdom about the nature of our humanity. (Lewis used the ancient term *Tao*, borrowed from Eastern thoughts, to name the way of life of these values.) He was concerned that the dominant worldviews of his twentieth-century propagated alternative values that would lead inevitably to the "abolition of man" (the title of a philosophical tract that he wrote on modern education). Lewis wrote his stories, including the *Chronicles*, as part of a strategy to rehabilitate the older values, and it was natural for him to draw in doing so on the imaginative resources and symbolic languages of this earlier, premodernist period. Like Tolkien, he was convinced that the future of the contemporary Western world would be exceedingly bleak without the vision of humanity embodied in them.

Chapter 3

TOLKIEN'S MYTHOPOESIS

Kirstin Johnson

In 1955 J. R. R. Tolkien wrote to his American publishers:

> I think the so-called "fairy story" one of the highest forms of litera-
> ture, and quite erroneously associated with children (as such). But my
> views on that I set out in a lecture delivered at St. Andrew's (on the
> Andrew Lang foundation. . .). I think it is quite an important work, at
> least for anyone who thinks me worth considering at all.

Tolkien then bemoaned that the "OUP has infuriatingly let it go out of
print, though it is now in demand—and my only copy has been stolen."[1]
The paper was put back in print, however, and well into his seventies
Tolkien continued to refer people to it, from his Middle-earth-editor-son,
Christopher, to *Hobbit* fans, his publishers, book critics, W. H. Auden—
even of his aged aunt. Consequently, St. Andrews University receives
frequent note in the collection of Tolkien's letters. In one of these letters
Tolkien writes:

> I must say I think the result of [this paper at St. Andrews] was entirely
> beneficial to *The Lord of the Rings*, which was a practical demonstration
> of the views that I expressed.[2]

"On Fairy-Stories" and the short story "Leaf by Niggle" were first combined to form the book *Tree and Leaf* in 1964. In 1988, Christopher Tolkien explains, the poem "Mythopoeia" was published for the first time in the collection as "[it] is closely related in its thought to a part of the essay . . . so much indeed that my father quoted 14 lines of the poem in the essay."[3] All three pieces, "Leaf by Niggle," "Mythopoeia," and "On Fairy-Stories" touch in different ways on what Tolkien calls "sub-creation." The essay and the story were written in the same period (1938–1939), but the poem "Mythopoeia" had initially been composed after a very significant discussion with C. S. Lewis almost a decade earlier.

The poem was dedicated to Lewis—a reflection on an evening's conversation. In his essay Tolkien refers to the poem as "a brief passage from a letter I once wrote to a man who described myth and fairy-story as 'lies,' though to do him justice he was kind enough and confused enough to call fairy-story making 'Breathing a lie through Silver.'"[4] This was a very different C. S. Lewis than the author and scholar he was to become. Until that night with Tolkien, Lewis was an avid *reader* of myths, but he could not believe that they could be anything more than, essentially, beautiful lies.

It is not Tolkien's poem itself that this paper will explore, but rather the concept that lies behind the poem and within its title: "Mythopoeia." It is a concept that, as Christopher Tolkien pointed out, is only touched upon in a part of Tolkien's essay, an essay full of challenging ideas.

Mythopoeic is a word and concept that Tolkien and Lewis thought and spoke much of, but used in print sparingly, as there were few—and, they fervently asserted, too few—cases that deserved the adjective. Today the word is virtually unknown in most circles and used to the point of meaninglessness in others. The latter tends to be in matters concerning the genre of fantasy and frequently with some connection to Tolkien. Often anything with a hint of "Middle-earth" in it is called *mythopoeic*.[5]

The most frequent definition to be found is "myth-making."[6] *Mythopoeia* or *mythopoesis* is often defined as "literary myth"—a definition that, particularly in consideration of the multiple definitions of myth, is not very helpful, which brings us back to Tolkien and his discussion of myth with Lewis. What did *they* understand the word to mean? To better understand this, we need to turn to Owen Barfield, who was a significant influence on both Tolkien and Lewis in their understanding of myth, language, and the mythopoeic.

Owen Barfield was one of the Inklings, the group of friends to which both Tolkien and Lewis belonged, and which convened regularly around beer and fireplaces to read aloud to each other, tell stories, argue, and discuss everything under the sun. Barfield and Lewis were the oldest friends in the group, having known each other as undergraduates. Becoming acquainted with Tolkien was a joy for both of them, as in him they found a mutual lover of language and of myth. It was not long before Tolkien shared some of his own created language and myth—a private endeavor since the age of eighteen—with Lewis. Lewis was delighted and later offered his highest praise by describing Tolkien to his oldest friend (Arthur Greeves) thus:

> The one man absolutely fitted, if fate had allowed, to be a third in our friendship in the old days, for he also grew up on William Morris and George MacDonald. Reading his fairy tale has been uncanny—it is so exactly like what we both have longed to write (or read) . . . describing the same world into which all three of us have the entry.[7]

Tolkien, upon acquaintance with Lewis and Barfield, was soon drawn into a longstanding discussion about language, myth, and imagination. Barfield's perspective was eventually published in two books: *History in English Words* in 1926 and *Poetic Diction* in 1928. While Tolkien was very much a man of his own opinions—"you might as well try to influence a bandersnatch" said Lewis—he did confide to Lewis that Barfield's concept of the "ancient semantic unity" of myth and language had "modified his whole outlook."[9]

Barfield had come to the conclusion that mythology definitely was *not* "a disease of language," as philologist Max Müller had called it (a refutation Tolkien reiterates in his essay "On Fairy-Stories"). Rather, it is "closely associated with the very origin of all speech and literature."[10] Put very simply, Barfield argued that initially for man, there had been no distinction between "literal" and "metaphorical." For example, when we translate the Latin *spiritus* we have to choose, using the context to aid us, between "spirit," "breath," or "wind." But early users of the language would not have felt the need to make distinctions. The blowing wind was not "like" someone breathing—it *was* the breath of a god.[11] Mythological stories were the same thing in narrative form. Nothing was "abstract" or "literal"; it was all one and the same. Barfield believed that this unity of consciousness had become fragmented as conceptual thinking developed, and he looked forward to man being better able to reconcile the literal and the abstract again some day with a renewed perception informed by the past, rather than reverting to it. There were aspects of Barfield's argument with which Tolkien and Lewis would never agree, but his "theory of how words originally embodied an ancient, unified perception inspired them both."[12]

Barfield, undoubtedly to Tolkien's delight, pointed out that "the general relation between language and myth" was "almost unfathomable," as is made clear by the very definition of the Greek *muthos*, which is also translated as "word."[13] Echoes of this resound in the voice of Tolkien's Treebeard: "Real names tell you the story of the things they belong to in my language."[14] Barfield elucidates in his *History in English Words*, explaining that the word *poetry* is from the Greek "to make." He repeats Philip Sidney's sixteenth-century explanation of a poet as "a maker"; rather than being someone who "merely follows nature," the poet brings forth new forms "such as never were in Nature," borrowing from nothing in existence, but ranging "into the divine consideration of what may be and should be." It is because the poet has contemplated the "Ideas" behind Nature that he thus "delivers forth, as he hath imagined them."[15] This finds resonance in "Mythopoeia," which claims: "We make still by the laws in which we're made."[16] The word *fiction*, Barfield adds, is from the Latin *fingere* to "form" or "make" implying "'making' or 'making up' purely imaginary forms" rather than "merely copying Nature . . . [and] the presence of a made-up element, especially when it comprised supernatural beings such as giants and fairies, was held to be one of the distinguishing marks of a *romance*."[17]

During the seventeenth century, the ranging "into the divine consideration" came to be understood as *invention*. From the Latin *invenire*, "to find," it was a word "implying that something had been found in Nature which had not yet been imitated by man." At the same time another word appeared: *creating*—"if poets could indeed spin their poetry entirely out of themselves, they were as '*creating* gods.'"[18] With this development Barfield reminds us of Joseph Addison's words: "This Talent of affecting the Imagination . . . has something in it like Creation: it bestows a kind of Existence, and draws up to the reader's view several objects which are not to be found in Being. It makes additions to Nature, and gives greater variety to God's works."[19]

Creare was one of those old Latin terms weighted with biblical associations; "its constant use in ecclesiastical Latin had saturated it with the special meaning of *creating*, in defined fashion, out of nothing, as opposed to the merely human making, which signified the rearrangement of matter already created, or the imitation of 'creatures.'"[20] The application of such a word to human activities would be called by Tolkien "sub-creating." Barfield points out that it is not surprising that some would call this blasphemy. Tolkien calls it an act of worship. What Addison described as giving "greater variety to God's works," Tolkien claims as a gift of assisting "in the effoliation and multiple enrichment of creation."[21] Up until the seventeenth century, Barfield claims, the word *inspiration* implied the understanding that "poets and prophets" were "direct mouthpieces of superior beings—beings such as the Muses." This concept began to suffer under men such as Hobbes, who scorned the concept that men were mere instruments "like a bagpipe," yet it nonetheless persisted. For Tolkien the concept still was potent. For him the distinction between the modern conception of *invention* (as opposed to the initial understanding explained by Barfield) and *inspiration* was important, for though he knew he was writing fiction, he says that he "had the sense of recording what was already 'there' . . . not of 'inventing.'"[22]

Although there is more of Barfield's exploration in which the relevance to Tolkien is both evident and pertinent, I will point out just one more word he addresses: *Faery*, spelled specifically in that manner. Barfield claims that this word expired in the time of Milton but was "resurrected in the nineteenth century"—and meant "not so much of an individual sprite as of a magic realm or state of being almost 'the whole supernatural element in romance.'"[23]

Barfield's study had modified Tolkien's outlook and had convinced Lewis that myth has a central place in language, literature, and the history of thought. Lewis had actually, in the midst of this process, become a theist. A conversation with Tolkien moved him significantly beyond this point, towards an acceptance of Christianity. And that was the conversation which inspired the poem "Mythopoeia."

Late into the evening of September 19, 1931—and well into the early hours of the next morning—Lewis, Tolkien, and another Inkling, Hugo Dyson, wandered the gardens and walks of Magdalene College. Their discussion was of metaphor and myth. Lewis described the evening a few days later to his old friend Greeves: "What Dyson and Tolkien showed me was this: that if I met the idea of sacrifice in a Pagan story I didn't mind it at all: again, that if I met the idea of a god sacrificing himself to himself . . . I liked it very much and was mysteriously moved by it: again, that the idea of the dying and reviving god (Balder, Adonis, Bacchus) similarly moved me provided I met it anywhere except in the Gospels. . . . Now [they have convinced me that] the story of Christ is simply a *true* myth: a myth working on us in the same way as the others, but with this tremendous difference that *it really happened.*"[24]

Tolkien had argued with Lewis that "not only the abstract thoughts of man but also his imaginative inventions must originate with God, and must in consequence reflect something of original truth."[25] Subcreating is actually fulfilling God's purpose, for we—to quote the poem—"make still by the laws in which we're made." Pagan myths have "something of the truth in them."[26] A myth, it was agreed, is "*a story out of which ever varying meanings will grow for different [recipients] in different ages.*"[27] "In the enjoyment of a great myth," a convinced Lewis would later expound, "[man] comes nearest to experiencing as a concrete what can otherwise be understood only as an abstraction. It is only while receiving the myth as a story that you can experience the principle correctly."[28] It is that experience of receiving the myth—that "story out of which ever varying meanings will grow"—which Tolkien calls *mythopoeia.* The uniqueness of the *Christian* myth, he explained to Lewis, is that God becomes the author, rather than man. The images he used were precise in location, in history, and in consequence: the old myth of a dying god had become fact. But, as Lewis came eventually to argue himself: "by becoming fact it does not cease to be myth: that is the miracle."[29]

The poem "Mythopoeia" is subtitled "from Philomythus to Misomythus" (from lover of myths to hater of myths) . . . for so Tolkien argues Lewis to be, if he can not allow for myths to contain a sense of Truth. If we are to apply Barfield's definition of *muthos* the barb goes deeper: "lover of words" to "hater of words." To use Lewis's accepted definition of myth it becomes "lover of meaning" and "hater of meaning." None of those negations would Lewis wish to own. In the poem Tolkien argues that a *relationship* with language allows man better to grasp the world that he inhabits. Readers of Lewis's *Voyage of the Dawn Treader*, who are familiar with Eustace's introduction to a star will note Tolkien's insistence that to call a star "a ball" of mathematically governed matter is not to know what a star is: "He sees no stars who does not see them first / of living silver made that sudden burst / to flame like flowers beneath an ancient song."[30] Understanding, names, and meaning are inextricably entwined.

On that walk Tolkien and Dyson had challenged Lewis that, if he was able to enjoy and receive from ancient Norse and Greek myths in a manner he could not with abstract arguments, would he not allow the same for a story they claimed to be true? "Could he not treat [the Christian story] as a *story*, be fully aware that he could draw nourishment from it which he could never find in a list of *abstract* truths?"[31] This Lewis pondered, and he found that he could. But Tolkien put forth yet another challenge: "If God chooses to be mythopoeic . . . shall we refuse to be mythopathic"?[32] Shall we refuse to enter and thus be transformed?

He reminds his medievalist friend what he should know well: that the authors he loves and teaches viewed Nature itself as God's story, God's poem. Man, part of the creation of that divine author, although "estranged" from the "only wise," is "not wholly lost"—in his bit of wisdom he is, or can be, a "sub-creator." In fact, Tolkien continues, man has a need to create, although he does not always do so in a fashion free from evil influence, for he does have free will. Tolkien goes so far as to suggest that it is the moral duty of man to "assert the existence of the good and the true, to seek truth through myth, to exercise his God-given function of sub-creation." He will have nothing of Lewis's purported world, "wherein no part / the little maker has with maker's art." Instead: "Blessed are the legend-makers with their rhyme / of things not found within recorded time. It is not they that have forgot the Night. . . ." They, he says, recognize Darkness and Death, but rather than retreat in despair, they turn to victorious song "and kindle hearts with legendary fire, / illuminating Now and dark Hath-been / with light of suns as yet by no man seen."[33] In this description are early intimations of the "loremaster" Aragorn.

"Blessed are the legend-makers, the sub-creators." Tolkien and Lewis both loved myth. They both had already attempted writing myths. Would Lewis be able to approach this gift anew as an *intentional* sub-creator, seeking to convey the mythopoeic? We know now, of course, that he did. Tolkien had convinced him. Those familiar with the writings of Lewis will know just how wholly he was converted to a "Philomythus." In a later article Lewis was so adamant as to write, "I hope everyone has read Tolkien's essay 'On Fairy Tales,' which is perhaps the most important contribution to the subject that anyone has yet made."[34] Elsewhere he would add: "it is indispensable."[35] Lewis proceeds to use the word *mythopoeic* more often than Tolkien, and he and Tolkien both feel the word is appropriate to use of *The Lord of the Rings* and *The Hobbit*. But Lewis helps us to understand that the word is not limited to that style of writing which they are content to call *fantasy*.

Lewis *does* talk of fantasy that is mythopoeic, but he also talks of other types of writing that attain this particular quality. It seems that while the medium of fantasy might be particularly conductive of the mythopoeic, that is not its only medium. Lewis expounds on the quality in greatest length in his *Anthology* of George MacDonald quotations, for MacDonald, Lewis felt, achieved the mythopoeic "better than any man" (though he did write this before the completion of *The Lord of the Rings*—perhaps he may have allowed Tolkien to share the laurel). Here Lewis argues that MacDonald's fantasy is mythopoeic in *nature*. Lewis is careful to make clear that this quality is something above and beyond the manner in which words are strung together; he is not always a great fan of MacDonald's grammatical ability and style.[36] Because of this, he ponders whether this art of "myth-making" can even be considered a "literary" art, for it seems that the form is only a medium. In his understanding of the mythopoeic, "the plot, the pattern of events," are crucial. The manner of conveyance is not. This is why the Ancient Norse story of Balder, so important to Lewis, Tolkien, *and* Barfield, is a great myth. For it was not a particular telling of the tale that was vital to their love of it, but the story itself that they loved. "Any means of communication whatever which succeeds in lodging those events in our imagination," says Lewis, "has done the trick." Of course it is desirable that the medium through which the story is conveyed is worthy, but even when it is not, the story will remain when the medium fades away.[37]

"The imagined events," says Lewis, "are the body and something inexpressible is the soul."[38] Lewis has come a long way from his insistence that all things that are real must therefore be rationally explicable. He now recognizes a place for "meaning-making" that cannot be catalogued. He laments, "It is astonishing how little attention critics have paid to story considered in itself"[39] . . . a lament Tolkien had been making for years in his studies on *Beowulf, Sir Gawain*, and other early literature.

Lewis says that this mythopoeic gift "may even be one of the greatest arts; for it produces works which give us (at the first meeting) as much delight and (on prolonged acquaintance) as much wisdom and strength as the works of the greatest poets. It is in some ways more akin to music than to poetry or at least to most poetry. It goes beyond the expression of things we have already felt . . . hits us at a level deeper than our thoughts . . ."[40] Tolkien echoes this. In searching around for what he calls "a less debatable word," Tolkien gives us *enchantment*. "Enchantment," he says, "produces a Secondary World into which both designer and spectator can enter, to the satisfaction of their senses while they are inside; but in its purity it is artistic in desire and purpose." He continues that "[to this] elvish craft . . . Fantasy aspires, and when it is successful" it is the greatest of human arts.[41] It is a place in which transformation can occur a transformation that does not fade upon reentry into the Primary World but, significantly, casts new light upon the Primary World. It is, in a sense, a medium of revelation. Tolkien and Lewis both turn us to the gospel story as the greatest example of the mythopoeic fairy tale. Indeed, it took Lewis some time to get over his frustration at how poorly crafted in terms of literature was the medium of the truest story four times over no less. Yet the very fact that the story was given four times over, and in a manner that left no question that the story itself was greater than the grammatical structures which conveyed it, gave credence to Tolkien's and Lewis's passion for story in and of itself and to their lament for its loss of esteem in the academy.

Tolkien and Lewis both practiced what Tolkien had preached. In their academic writings, lectures, and tutorials they sought to draw people back to the initial story in the texts they were studying. But they also sought to "make by the law in which they were made" and create mythopoeia themselves. Tolkien's results, named the "Book of the 20th Century" was apparently the most read book in that century other than the Bible.[42] For more than two hundred years, that place had been held by John Bunyan's *Pilgrim's Progress*. Tolkien wrote that *The Lord of the Rings* was the "practical demonstration of the view that [he had] expressed" in "On Fairy-Stories."[43] Rereading *The Lord of the Rings* with that in mind will reveal just how very explicitly Tolkien did express those views, how highly he held mythopoeia.

The book begins with a Middle-earth from which story is rapidly being lost. One of Bilbo's distinguishing features is that he is both a story collector and a storyteller: a story lover. The reason Frodo, Sam, Pippin, and Merry are able to journey (Tolkien repeatedly reminds us) is because they have benefited from Bilbo's love of stories and likewise love those stories. Although they, like all hobbits, also love stories about themselves, there is something more in many of Bilbo's tales. Knowing and believing in elves, for instance, not only makes these hobbits somehow different from other hobbits but also causes them to look about with different eyes. In each place of rest and restoration along the journey, Tolkien makes clear that part of the essential nourishment that the hobbits receive is story—in word and in song, and even in picture. The stories given in places such as Bombadil's home and Rivendell fortify them and, we are explicitly told, increase their understanding of Nature and the world—and thus of themselves. Rivendell, Tolkien wrote, "represents Lore—the preservation in reverent memory of all tradition concerning the good, wise, and beautiful . . . [it is] not a scene of *action* but of *reflection*. Thus it is a place visited on the way to all deeds or adventures."[44] Elrond, he said, symbolized "the ancient wisdom"; he is "greatest of lore-masters."[45] Gandalf, of course, is renowned for his knowledge of stories, and it is in his studies of such—even when in bits and pieces—that the danger of the Ring comes truly to be known. At times different members of the Fellowship are able to produce significant pieces of information that aid the Quest, precisely because they know a story the others do not. Not surprisingly, the scholar of ancient European legends (many of which exist only in part) reminds us repeatedly that even the fragments of stories are to be treasured and remembered; thus, lore-masters such as Elrond, Gandalf, and Aragorn must know languages too. Indeed, it is due to the loss of ancient languages that the tale of Isildur has been forgotten in the libraries of Gondor.[46] Celeborn, "the wisest of elves," propounds: "Do not despise the lore that has come down from distant years: for oft it may chance that old wives keep in memory word of things that once were needful for the wise to know."[47] And thus a fragment of a rhyme, "repeat[ed] without understanding" by an "old wife" in Gondor, teaches Gandalf of the healing powers of the wild herb *kingsfoil*—thus saving the lives of Faramir, Eowyn, and Merry.

Aragorn is, of course, a crucial source of stories—and thus of wisdom—to the Fellowship, and it is through him that Tolkien explicitly impresses upon us that even fragments of tales may convey the mythopoeic. Tolkien puts into Aragorn's mouth the fragment most dear to him: the Lay of Beren and Luthien. Appropriately, it was this incomplete love story about the ancestors of Arwen and Aragorn, whose elf and human courtship paralleled their own, that first revealed Tolkien's gift of the mythopoeic to Lewis.[49]

In Tolkien's epic it is clear that a lover of story will aid the battle for good, and a hoarder of story, such as Saruman or even Denethor, will hinder it—so too will a scorner of story, such as Boromir. Tolkien goes to some length to make clear that Boromir, brave and good as his initial intent might be, severely handicaps the Fellowship because he "care[d] little for lore, save the tales of old battles." Faramir was "otherwise in mind . . . a lover of lore and of music, and therefore by many in those days his courage was judged less than his brother's. But it was not so. . . . He welcomed Gandalf at such time as he came to the City, and he learned what he could from his wisdom."[50] We are told this a number of times—even by Faramir himself, who loved his brother dearly but knew that Boromir's lack of concern for anything but "battle and glory" might lead to downfall.[51] It is crucially significant to understand why the one *man* who is given the opportunity to take the Ring is not even tempted. Here, I think, the film of the book does fail us. For it is important to Tolkien that the reader understands that Faramir has truly learned what he explains to Frodo: that "such things do not breed peace—*not if aught may be learnt from ancient tales* . . . ancient tales teach us also the peril of rash words concerning such things as [the Ring]."[52] Faramir has been formed by ageless truths and meanings in the stories Gandalf has shown him and in the others he has explored on his own. He is able to believe in things no man he knows has seen—such as the perilous, enchanting elves—and he has gained the wisdom of experience *within* story to discern that, regardless of intentions, the Ring *will* corrupt. He is, as he says, "wise enough to know that there are some perils from which a man should flee."[53] He does not even wish to see it. In significant contrast with his brother, Faramir parts ways with Frodo expressing hope that some day they will be able to retell their tales together, and Frodo responds: "To have found [your friendship] turns evil to great good."[54] The rulers of men may be failing—Gondor's Denethor hoarding his stories, his libraries in dust; Théoden scorning stories, his tapestries hid in shadows—but we see hope in their heirs. Eomer believes the tales Aragorn speaks of, and wants to learn more. Faramir knows his tales so well that he will make a splendid steward of Gondor and never wish for the throne that is not his.

And into the mouth of the awakened Théoden, Tolkien puts one of his strongest passions. After Gandalf chides him for not recognizing the Ents—"Is it so long since you listened to tales by the fireside? There are children in your land who [would know them even from] twisted threads of stories"—Théoden responds: "Out of the shadows of legend I begin to understand the marvel of the trees I think. . . . We cared little for what lay beyond the borders of our land. Songs we have that tell of these things, but we are forgetting them, teaching them only to children, as a careless custom."[55]

"Banished to the nursery" you will hear Tolkien lament in "On Fairy-Stories"—that which is essential sustenance and fortification for man; that which once warriors demanded to hear. But the Tree of Tales does not fade: "The old that is strong does not wither / Deep roots are not reached by the frost," although its leaves may get covered in dust and its branches hid by shadows.[56] Now that the shadows are being shed from the legends of Rohan, Théoden is having his understanding even of Nature illuminated and transformed.

The Lord of the Rings ends with Sam, who loves stories and who is wise enough in his innocence to understand that he and Frodo are *in* a story that is but a leaf on a "branch on the Tree of Tales."[57] For Tolkien, Sam's "disquisition on the seamless web of Story" was one of the most moving parts of the book.[58] Once their quest has ended, Sam is commissioned by Frodo with a weighty charge—a charge that will guard the Shire against Théoden's lament of "tales forgotten." Sam must read aloud out of the *Red Book*, which contains both the *Tale of the Ring* and extracts from *Books of Lore* from Rivendell. He must thus "keep alive the memory of the age that is gone, so that people will remember the Great Danger and so love their beloved land all the more. And that [and gardening!] will keep you as busy and as happy as anyone can be, as long as your part of the story goes on."[59] There are echoes here of an old text Tolkien knew well: "Watch yourself closely so that you do not forget the things your eyes have seen or let them slip from your heart as long as you live. Teach them to your children and to their children after them . . . teach [my words] to your children, talking about them when you sit at home and when you walk along the road, when you lie down and when you get up."[60] Sam will be sharing with his children and his people stories of the ages, which will transform as they are experienced by their listeners, and which will *continue* to transform. "Ever varying meanings, which will grow" as the listeners travel a "road that goes ever on."

Sam has a happy commission, for he has a story to steward that is *more* than fantasy or fairy tale—it is also mythopoeia. If not for everyone, certainly for millions, this particular tale has produced an artistic "Secondary World into which [they] can enter, to the satisfaction of their senses while they are inside." The images and events are permanently lodged within many, who continue to visit the story, in text, in visuals, in memory—ever experiencing varying and sometimes transforming meanings, even in such little yet profound ways as how, like Théoden, they see a tree. Tolkien's tale has "effoliated and multiplied enrichment of creation" for a few generations now, and seems likely to continue to do so. C. S. Lewis wrote that it would be wonderful if *The Lord of the Rings* "really succeeded in selling," for "it would inaugurate a new age. Dare we hope?"[61] It is perhaps possible to assert that such a thing has happened. "Fantasy/fairy tale," the genre Tolkien sees as most likely to attain the mythopoeic, has never held such wide acclaim in either the popular or the academic eye [as it does today]. Well, perhaps I should amend that . . . has not for a few centuries. It will be interesting to see who will now move to assent with Tolkien and Lewis, and who will continue to dissent. "Story considered in itself" was their challenge. Those of us, particularly of English literature and theology departments, are "lore-masters" of our time and place. Are we learning and sharing it? Allowing for others to experience the mythopoeic of which "something inexpressible is the soul"? Or will we hoard it, use it for our own purposes, or remain more interested in battle than in story?

Chapter 4

TOLKIEN, CREATION, AND CREATIVITY

Trevor Hart

"We make still by the law in which we're made."[1]

If some of the most distinctive ideas in J. R. R. Tolkien's essay "On Fairy-Stories" were only born and clarified in his mind in 1938–1939 as he sat down to compose his Andrew Lang Lecture for St. Andrews University, others had already received an earlier, less conceptually developed airing throughout the 1930s, for example, in the poem "Mythopoiea" and the 1936 lecture "*Beowulf*: The Monsters and the Critics."[2] Some, though, go back much further even than this, finding artistic expression in Tolkien's earliest literary ventures. One particular theological note, I shall suggest, is sounded clearly in this primeval dawn, and from then on it undergirds the whole of Tolkien's literary output like a reverberating ground bass.

In September 1954 Tolkien drafted a response to a Roman Catholic correspondent who had queried whether in certain elements of *The Lord of the Rings* Tolkien had not stepped beyond the boundaries proper to artistic imagination, effectively trespassing upon matters of "metaphysics" that ought either to have been treated differently or else accorded dignified silence. In his reply, Tolkien made what on the face of it seems to be a remarkable claim—namely, that the nature of "the relation of

Creation to making and sub-creation" is what "the whole matter" of his literary output "from beginning to end" had been "mainly concerned with."[3] The claim is striking because its tone suggests not just an author who, looking back over his career, realizes that earlier works can already be seen to contain hints and anticipations of concerns that emerge with force and clarity only in his more mature writings. That would hardly be surprising at all. What Tolkien says, though, points to a sustained, self-conscious and deliberate concern with a singular theological and aesthetic question, the importance of which had haunted him from the outset and never left him, and in terms of which his oeuvre as a whole, therefore, might at one level be made sense of.[4] Briefly stated it is this: if human artistry is creative and powerful, what relationship does it have to that other "creativity" which Christian faith ascribes properly to God alone? Are we in any sense, to cite the maxim of Paul Gauguin, creators "like unto our Divine Master"?[5] And if not, if clear blue theological water needs to be opened up between us and God at this point, what place remains then for an understanding of artistic imagination as a genuinely "creative" engagement with things, rather than an essentially mimetic following or echoing of something unequivocally "given" in the divinely created ordering of the world? Tolkien understood only too well the fact that, for Christians who grappled with this subject, certain parts of the map were clearly marked with the legend "Here be dragons!" and not without good reason. Corpses littered the ground of the nineteenth-century Romanticism that was his own heritage, bearing witness to earlier failed attempts to engage its more Promethean spirits in the service of a Christian theology and poetics. Dragons, though, of theological or other sorts, held no fear for Tolkien, as long as they were handled carefully and well. And he ventured forth, determined to tame rather than to slay these particular dragons if at all possible. The attempt to do precisely this lies identifiably at the center of the 1939 lecture "On Fairy-Stories," where Tolkien introduces and develops the distinctive notion of artistry as "sub-creation." In this essay, though, I shall trace other forays into the same territory, bearing weapons and wearing armor of a different sort. Sub-creation, as we shall see, is already present in all but name in the beginning, and within the context of Tolkien's own imaginative bids to call a world into being.

"AND GOD SAW THAT IT WAS GOOD": MYTH, CREATIVITY, AND CONSTRAINT

The Silmarillion opens with a creation myth. There is, we might suppose, nothing very surprising in this as such. After all, if one is going to have such a myth for the sake of literary verisimilitude, then one may as well put it at the beginning, which is where such things are generally to be found. But there is much more to it than this. "Ainulindalë" is no mere aesthetic "book-end," and it comes first not just in order to keep the narrative chronology intact, but because in a profound sense it provides the clue for understanding all that follows thereafter—namely, Tolkien's vast imaginative enterprise as a whole.[6] "Not only is ["Ainulindalë"] one of his most original and beautiful pieces of writing," Ralph Wood suggests, but it "also serves as the foundation for everything else."[7] As in Tolkien's own Christian faith, so, too, in his literary output the theme of "creation" is not just concerned with explaining beginnings but with making sense of the whole from beginning to end. The key notes which are shot identifiably through the pattern of Middle-earth and its story ring here already in its primordial moment; and not faintly, but sounded with all the urgency of the horns of Rohan. The story of creaturely existence, and the struggle between good and evil that lies at its heart, is, Tolkien suggests, no more and no less than the story of creaturely participation in the creative venture of God; and in saying so, he does not have Middle-earth alone in mind.

We should note at once, though, Tolkien's creation myth is not an allegorical rendering of its Christian counterpart, and attempts to read it as such are likely only to mislead. Tolkien consistently resisted enthusiastic attempts by his readers to interpret The Lord of the Rings as an allegory, a resistance already heralded in his early critical works. Myths, legends, and fairy stories, he insists, are not allegories, and should not be treated as such. They are precisely stories, and while they certainly resonate with "realities" and "truths" of various sorts existing beyond their own borders—and in ways to which the critic must attend—more fundamentally what they are about is not something else, but precisely themselves.[8] Both the sentiment and the theoretical underpinning for it echo George MacDonald's views, though Tolkien does not cite him as a source.[9] Not only is literary art not primarily mimetic with respect to "Primary

Reality," both men insist, neither is it to be viewed as essentially *symbolic*, as if understanding it means "decoding" some arcane point-for-point correlation in which its various elements "stand for" other things rather than being important in their own right. On the contrary, Tolkien urges, stories must stand (or fall) first and foremost on their own terms, as the narration of particular happenings and individual characters. This does not mean that stories are (or could ever be) wholly divorced from what, in "On Fairy-Stories," Tolkien refers to as "Primary Reality." Indeed, he insists, inasmuch as they actually contain "life" (are related in one way or another to something we may identify as "real"), all decent stories will in fact contain particular events that evoke wider patterns of experience or individual characters who embody traits of a "universal" sort.[10] This is simply a function of the proper relationship between particulars and universals in the nature of things and the meaningful order that the patterns of created reality manifest. And the better written a deliberate allegory is, for its part, the more it will stand up to scrutiny in its own right as story. Thus "[a]llegory and story converge, meeting somewhere in Truth. So that the only perfectly consistent allegory is a real life; and the only fully intelligible story is an allegory. . . . But the two start out from opposite ends."[11] The fact that particulars within stories inevitably *contain* such universal elements, therefore, does not mean that their literary function is simply to *represent* them.[12] In stories, as in life, things are primarily what they are, and they should be judged as such.

Given all this, we should hardly expect to find in Tolkien's "elvish" creation myth a crudely disguised allegory of the biblical account in Genesis 1–3, though we might be equally surprised not to discover some basic resonances between the two. In fact, Tolkien draws on a wide range of legendary sources for inspiration, and in certain respects the detail of his own story has more in common with the "theologies" of Nordic and classical myth. He deliberately casts his own imaginary world, we must remember, in a remote pre-Christian and pre-Jewish stage of earth's past, a move which frees him conveniently from expectations of finding any close correlations between the religious outlooks of the two stages, while yet leaving the truth (as he certainly saw it) of the Christian "myth"—as yet (i.e., in Middle-earth) to be revealed— unscathed. So Caldecott's judgment that Tolkien "was trying to write an account that would be complementary to, while not contradicting, the Genesis story"[13] seems more appropriate, than Tom Shippey's description of it as a "calque" on Genesis.[14] The latter reading tends to create false expectations, leading us to inquire about direct correspondences or to worry unduly, perhaps, about the presence of elements of apparent polytheism in his myth.[15] In fact, there are probably none in any case (Tolkien's "Ainur" are unambiguously created by Eru, and therefore at most demi-gods); but that is not the point. The point is that, even if there *were* traces of polytheism here, one might argue that this would not much matter, any more than the existence of polytheism in *actual* historical religions pre-dating Christianity "matters" where judgments about the truth of the latter are concerned.

This (essentially literary) point, though, while important, can only be pressed so far in Tolkien's case. For there certainly *were* things that mattered to him in this way and applied a brake to his sense of imaginative licence. If indeed, in Caldecott's terms, a hierarchy of created angelic sub-creators did not *contradict* the Christian faith to which Tolkien himself subscribed but *complemented* it, one can nonetheless imagine things that *would* contradict it in ways Tolkien himself felt to be wholly inappropriate. And it is clear that he was conscious of a deep sense of artistic responsibility at certain points. Responsibility, that is, not so much to his church and its creeds as to the basic nature of reality as he believed it to be, and as the artist, therefore, was obliged to attend to it. "(I)n every world on every plane," he would write later, "all must ultimately be under the Will of God."[16] While he felt free to call into existence imaginary worlds of sorts that varied greatly in their particulars (even their religious particulars) from the actual world he knew, he felt no freedom to tinker with certain fundamentals, and this deep theological conviction about divine sovereignty (and thus the ultimate goodness of reality itself) seems to have been among them.[17] His casting of "Ainulindalë," the Elvish myth of creation, therefore, while free in many respects, was nonetheless not capriciously or completely free but constrained in certain basic ways. It is important to grasp this because in this sense the myth itself was, as we shall see, an example of precisely the sort of "creativity" that it itself explores and depicts, and which Tolkien believed to be the essence of *human* creativity at its best.

And here, surely, is difference on the large scale if we are concerned to find it: for whereas the biblical myth has singularly to do with God's creativity, "Ainulindalë," I shall suggest, is concerned also with setting *our* creaturely creativity in proper theological perspective and points to a relationship between them in which both unity and distinction are vital.

"EA! LET THESE THINGS BE!": ART AS CREATED CREATIVITY

"There was Eru, the One, who in Arda is called Ilúvatar; and he made first the Ainur, the Holy Ones, that were the offspring of his thought, and they were with him before aught else was made."[18] So Tolkien's myth begins. It tells the story of the participation of the Ainur—created angelic beings or demi-gods—in Ilúvatar's own creation of the world of Middle-earth. That Ilúvatar is himself the sole originating source of all things and remains sovereign in his authority over all things is clear from beginning to end, but he chooses to create the world through a form of shared and responsive creativity. He has, we recall, already created the Ainur themselves, so this inclusive and participative mode is clearly a matter of choice on his part rather than necessity. And it is a choice fraught with both exciting possibilities and attendant dangers and risks with which Ilúvatar himself will have duly to deal. Since he elects nonetheless to pursue this route, we must assume that the dangers are outweighed by the supposed potential goods.

The metaphor in terms of which the myth pictures this creative interplay is, appropriately, an artistic one. Ilúvatar propounds a great musical theme, and invites the Ainur to join in the music-making, each adorning the main theme with his own, to the end of a great and glorious harmony sounding forth. The creativity of the Ainur, therefore, is quite unlike Ilúvatar's own. While each is free to fashion his own individual melody, the skill or "art" of the matter lies not in any sheer creativity *ex nihilo* but precisely in the harmonious development of a theme that Ilúvatar himself has already propounded, which determines, as it were, the form of the overall work. The core image, then, is that of harmonizing by free and spontaneous ornamentation. For his part, Ilúvatar will "sit and hearken, and be glad that through you great beauty has been wakened into song."[19] And so it is, for a time at least. There is a "great music" in the heavens, one which not only satisfies Ilúvatar but "goes out into the Void" so that it is no longer void—a music that, for a while, contains no flaws. "But as the theme progressed, it came into the heart of Melkor to interweave matters of his own imagining that were not in accord with the theme of Ilúvatar; for he sought therein to increase the power and glory of the part assigned to himself."[20] Melkor is the most gifted among the Ainur, and thus his capacity for generating disharmony is also greatest. There follows what to all intents and purposes is a competition between Melkor's repeated attempts to weave discord into the grand design and Ilúvatar's responses to the same. The latter become less "playful" and more awe-inspiring as the exchange progresses, and it all ends in the triumph of Ilúvatar bringing about a shattering harmonious climax before the music ceases as abruptly as it had all begun.

We should note several things about this mythical treatment of what, in Christian terms, would be described as the Fall of creation and the entry of evil into God's world (though, again, we must grant the elves' account of it its own integrity rather than forcing it too quickly or easily into a Christian mould).

- First (in Miltonic rather than biblical fashion) the myth locates the primordial rebellion not among God's human creatures but earlier, prior to the appearance of human and elvish life, among the angelic beings who are God's "primary" creation in chronological terms at least.
- Second, while the seriousness of "discord" (evil) and its implications is certainly not underplayed, it is clear from beginning to end in the myth that Ilúvatar is and remains sovereign with respect to it, and there is never any suggestion that the cosmos might finally be the site of a dualistic struggle between equally matched principles of light and darkness, good and evil, no matter how dark things may actually become at times from a creaturely perspective. This qualification is important, since at one level dualism and its attendant uncertainties are clearly more attractive from a literary point of view. We are more likely to keep reading, after all, if the outcome of the action is unknown than if everything appears simply to be unfolding in accordance

with some predetermined grand design. If, in his narration of the history of Middle-earth, Tolkien is able to keep us turning page after page, it is because in his fiction, as in life, contingency is certainly everywhere apparent, the outcomes of particular events or even larger patterns of events being far from evident at the point of their occurrence (or, perhaps, even from the writer's perspective, at the point of their generation in his mind's eye). Yet in asking and answering questions on the cosmic scale, Tolkien ascribes to the elves the same deep conviction that characterized his own Christian faith; namely, that despite multitudinous appearances to the contrary, reality has its ultimate creative source in goodness, and goodness will finally prevail in the face of challenges to it. That it is not yet clear when or how this may happen or what precisely may occur en route (ultimate triumph is entirely compatible with many penultimate defeats and struggles, as Christian eschatology is all too aware) enables this metaphysical conviction to be held together nonetheless with a genuine sense of freedom, unpredictability, and literary excitement.

- Third, goodness and evil as manifested in God's creatures are each construed in the myth in terms of a form of subordinate creativity or artistry. Both terms of this phrase are important. What Ilúvatar calls the Ainur to do involves the exercise of freedom and the skillful adornment of his own prior artistic work. Each is invited to bring into existence something that has hitherto enjoyed no existence, and thereby to enhance the overall sound of the music. And yet this is clearly not an act of creation in the same sense that the word may be used of Ilúvatar's own prior activity. He "originates" in a much more basic sense, calling into being the Ainur themselves and the fundamental theme in accordance with which they are called now to make music. And, as already noted, he remains master of the music, able to bring it to artistic fulfilment despite serious attempts to disrupt or spoil it. So, the creativity of the Ainur is clearly subordinate or (to use Tolkien's own preferred term) sub-creation, and this takes the forms both of a responsible and respectful creativity—making music in accord with Ilúvatar's own design and the fruitful possibilities pregnant within it—in which creaturely vocation is, as it were, fulfilled; and an irresponsible and disrespectful (insubordinate) "creativity" that, in its pursuit of autonomy and self-glorification, succeeds only in a temporary spoiling of what Ilúvatar has made. What Melkor seeks (but can never have precisely because he is creature not Creator) is a form of creativity like unto Ilúvatar's own. What he and the other Ainur are called to instead is participation in a corresponding form of "creaturely creativity" proper to their own being and also a genuine participation in the shaping of God's world, not merely passive reception or indwelling of it.

- Fourth, it is by a superior artistry that is, as it were, able to redeem disharmony rather than overwhelm it that Ilúvatar triumphs. He does not, unlike the God of at least one Christian hymn, "drown . . . all music but his own,"[21] but rather takes it up into the pattern of his own music-making, whether by endorsing its own positive contribution to that music or by making such adjustments to the overall pattern that any intended discord is skillfully reconfigured to serve the greater beauty.[22] What Melkor discovers, in fact, is that rebellion is futile, since "no theme may be played that hath not its uttermost source in me, nor can any alter the music in my despite. For he that attempteth this shall prove but mine instrument in the devising of things more wonderful, which he himself hath not imagined."[23] Indeed, it is true of the Ainur generally that, while they "know much," they cannot see the full meaning even of their own creative contribution to the world, that being hidden in the larger scheme of things known only, as yet, to Ilúvatar himself. Not only is the provenance of all creaturely creativity (including, we note without further comment here, its deliquent and evil manifestations[24]) to be located in the complex plenitude of what Ilúvatar himself has called into existence; so, too, he remains creative throughout and feeds into the dynamic pattern of the world new and unanticipated (i.e., by the Ainur) elements that, in their turn, call forth further creative responses from the creaturely side.

- A fifth point is worthy of brief mention for reasons that will become apparent duly. The "vision" sounded forth in Ilúvatar's music and duly enhanced by the "sub-creative" minstrelsy of the Ainur is not yet the creation of the world itself, but rather the casting of its primordial blueprint. For the world itself to be born, a further, uniquely divine prerogative must be exercised by Ilúvatar himself. Thus, we read: "Ilúvatar called to them, and said: "I know the desire of your minds that what ye have seen shall verily be, not only in your thought, but even as ye yourselves are, and yet other. Therefore I say: Eä! Let these things Be!"[25]

"ULTIMATELY OF THE SAME STUFF": ART AND THE "MIGHTY THEME" OF GOD

What we have here, then, is a theological myth depicting the creation of the world by God and the participation in God's creative activity by angelic beings whose own mode of creativity is decisively marked by the fact that they are, in their turn, God's creatures rather than his divine counterparts. In the casting of this myth, though, Tolkien is doing more than furnishing an imaginary cosmogony in terms of which the history of Middle-earth might be framed. He is exploring a central aesthetic and theological idea that, I have suggested, concerned him throughout his writing career—namely, the nature and place of creaturely creativity in relation to God's own unique creative prerogatives and activity with respect to the world. "History often resembles Myth," he wrote in 1939, "because they are both ultimately of the same stuff."[26] It was not a flippant observation, nor just a casual allusion to the fact that, in some sense, all myth and fantasy (all human imagining indeed) must begin with the raw materials of the everyday reality that we know, however far it may duly depart from it. Something deeper is at stake, something about the relationships pertaining between primary and secondary realities, and the inexorable gravitational pull of the one on all our dealings with the other. At almost every point in his writing Tolkien deliberately blurs the boundaries between the two, and while, as Shippey notes, it would be easy enough to dismiss this as mere whimsy and even personal delusion[27] (his "great desire" for dragons having finally got the better of common sense, as it were), we should probably see it instead as a deliberate literary strategy of disorientation and destabilization, causing us regularly to question the location of the boundaries and their significance for our transport in the respective territories they mark out. Middle-earth may be a "fantasy" world in all sorts of important and proper senses, but Tolkien was quite deliberate, we recall again, in casting his epic story firmly within the prehistoric geography of our own world. And what he tells us about it, while far from being allegorical, nonetheless has our world constantly in its sights. Tolkien's understanding of artistic creativity demands that it should, since (like all art) Middle-earth can only ever be an elaboration and development of a "mighty theme" first propounded by the one creator of all things in heaven and on earth. Or, in the terms of the essay "On Fairy-Stories," genuine sub-creative art (rather than mere "magic"), while it may result in secondary realities which are wholly unlike the "Primary World," is nonetheless always faithful to that same world and issues from a love of and respect for it. That "Ainulindalë" itself is not an account of the creation of some far-flung world but an ancient elvish account of the creation of our own world further encourages us to look to it expecting to find in it not just something alien, but something of "the same stuff." And what we find is an exploration, all the more easily handled, perhaps, because it is cast in fictional rather than straightforwardly religious and theological terms of the nature of human artistry vis-à-vis God's own distinctive role as creator. In the story of the Ainur, that is to say, we see how Tolkien thinks not just about some mythical angelic artistry, but about his own and ours that are "ultimately of the same stuff." And these thoughts, as it turns out, reach back all the way to his earliest commission of ideas to paper.

HOW IT WAS "IN THE BEGINNING"

The version of "Ainulindalë" to which I have alluded above was not cast in its final form until the early 1950s, when the bulk of Tolkien's literary engagement with the history of Middle-earth was already extant, but its earliest version reaches back more than thirty years to the imaginative genesis of Middle-earth itself. According to Tolkien's own later recollection, it was while he was in Oxford, having only recently returned from the First World War, and employed on the staff of the New English Dictionary[28] that he wrote "a cosmogonical myth, 'The Music of the Ainur,' defining the relation of The One, the transcendental creator, to the Valar, the 'Powers,' the angelical First-created, and their part in ordering and carrying out the Primeval Design."[29] While this first draft was certainly developed and modified over the years,[30] what is striking for our purposes is the presence already in its most primitive form of all the basic elements outlined above: the essential distinction between Ilúvatar and the Ainur, the call of Ilúvatar to his angelic creatures to share responsibly in bringing his world (his heart's "mighty design"[31]) into being through the artistry of music-making, the rebellion of Melkor (or "Melko" as he is in this early version) through a form of "vain imagining," and the sovereign triumph of Ilúvatar over evil by redeeming rather than crushing it.

Here already, then, at the very outset of Tolkien's own artistic career we find him wrestling in mythic form with the place of the artist and artistry in God's world; or, as he would express it later in correspondence reflecting on his oeuvre, "the relation of Creation to making and sub-creation," "the problem of the relation of Art (and Sub-creation) and Primary Reality."[32] As yet these were categories still to be born in his mind, but the vital questions (and in broad terms the answers to which, intuitively, he was drawn) were already there in the beginning, and they remained with him to the end. Creaturely creativity could never be confused with God's own, yet it was a full and responsible activity that was, in some clear sense, a matter of world-making, and no mere passive receptivity of something absolutely given. If anything, this emphasis on the definite contribution that artistry makes to God's world is more forcefully articulated in earlier recensions of the myth than in later ones. Thus, for instance, the original draft has Ilúvatar speaking clearly to the Ainur of a creation as yet related only in outline form, with empty spaces left deliberately unfilled and adornments unrealized, existing only in the hidden depths of Ilúvatar's own imagination. This lack of completeness is not, though, a lack in any ultimate sense but rather an opportunity, a vocational charge, indeed, laid upon the Ainur to take the theme that has been propounded to them and adorn it with their own thoughts and imaginative enhancements.[33]

Twenty years or so later, in his first identifiable revision of the text,[34] this emphasis was less expansively developed, but still clear. Ilúvatar's music, as delared to the Ainur, is as yet avowedly "incomplete" and "unadorned," and looks for its enrichment and fulfilment to the creative contributions of the Ainur themselves as they exercise their God-given powers of artistry.[35] By the time Tolkien revised the myth again[36] even this language had disappeared, and a new motif, the unparalleled moment when Ilúvatar grants actual existence to the imaginations of all their hearts, had been introduced.[37] This "central shift" in the myth (as Christopher Tolkien calls it[38]) seems unlikely to reflect tinkering with the order of an imaginary cosmogony for reasons of a purely literary or aesthetic sort (the pursuit of a more satisfying "pattern") alone. Again, I suggest, we should understand Tolkien's struggle for appropriate order as one of an altogether more fundamental sort, and hold his mythology closely together with corresponding developments in his thinking about the place of human artistry within the context of a divine creation. The decade lying between the two versions was the very one during which Tolkien's most deliberate and sustained reflection on these themes occurred, as he embarked on the creative venture that turned into *The Lord of the Rings*; we find the most direct reflection of the direction his thought took in the essay "On Fairy-Stories," written and reworked for publication during the same period. The adjustments to the text of "Ainulindalë" do not, strictly speaking, reflect or effect any change of substance, but they serve emphatically to clarify and to underline certain things. Perhaps, as Tolkien reflected on things, unashamed talk of the Ainur's artistry as called upon to "complete" Ilúvatar's world now seemed to risk an unacceptable blurring of the boundaries between divine and creaturely prerogatives, thereby drawing ironically close to the heart of Melko's sin itself. When "creative desire" is wedded to mortality, he ruminated later, it is always in danger of a "Fall" akin to Melko's. "It may become possessive, clinging to the things made as its own, the sub-creator wishes to be the Lord and God of his private creation."[39]

That artistry among creatures does not and must never be supposed to entail any form of "[c]reating like unto our Divine Master" is something about which Tolkien appears never to have had any doubt, but the importance of keeping the essential difference between them clear at all times appears to have impressed itself upon him more heavily when he turned eventually to organize his own thoughts on the matter, a task provoked by the invitation from St. Andrews to deliver an Andrew Lang Lecture.[40] Certainly, the net effect of the changes he made to the myth between versions B and C is to prise created and "uncreated" creativity apart again quite decisively, insisting that when the Ainur have done their utmost and their best, their imaginings yet lack the vital thing— existence, being, life itself. Only Ilúvatar may grant them that, and apart from his endorsement of them and his creative speaking of them into existence, they remain lacking in reality.[41] Thus the absolute reliance of the Ainur's creative contribution not just on Ilúvatar's prior activity (as though this needed in some sense to be "finished off" or "made good" by someone else's independent contribution) but equally upon his continuing presence and action in, with, and under theirs (apart from which it all amounts to nothing) is driven home far more fully than in earlier versions.

Man, Tolkien ruminates in "On Fairy-Stories," is most truly an artist when what he makes goes identifiably beyond representations or symbolic interpretations of the world in which he finds himself (important and powerful though these may be) and brings forth new form.[42] This begins at the simple level of "meddling" with the Primary World,[43] taking its familiar configurations of shape and color and sound and reordering them, glimpsing new possibilities that serve to arrest and to delight us. So this is never *creatio ex nihilo*; and yet the artist is reality's respectful lover rather than her slave. Art is, after all, art, and a tale a tale, intended first and foremost to have literary effect. And "liberation 'from the channels the creator is known to have used already' is the fundamental function of 'sub-creation,' a tribute to the infinity of His potential variety, one of the ways in which indeed it is exhibited."[44] Artistic making, therefore, departs freely, properly, and often from the constraints of whatever appears to be given in the world; but when it does so its end is never selfish,[45] always being rooted in a delight in the world for its own sake and desiring nothing more than the world's own good, its enhancement, and the fulfilment of possibilities latent within it. And this remains true even though, paradoxically, art's most powerful and sustained trysts with reality result in the bringing to birth not just of isolated objects but whole imaginative worlds within which those same objects belong and make sense and have their being. It is the capacity for imaginative vision on this larger scale, in fact, to which Tolkien refers as "sub-creation." Done well (with genuine art), such imagining captures something of "the inner consistency of reality" even as it displaces it. It draws us quickly into its alternative world, granting us an appropriate form of "Secondary Belief" for the duration of our transport there. Done badly, it results in a circumstance, Tolkien notes wryly, in which our disbelief has "not so much to be suspended as hung, drawn, and quartered."[46] The inculcation of secondary belief, he suggests, is an ancient elvish craft—enchantment—aspired to but never fully realized by human imagining in this world, though fantasy is the genre that perhaps comes closest to it. As he formulated such thoughts as these, Tolkien's own latest "experiment in the arts of . . . inducing 'Secondary Belief'"[47] was already being drafted. We may suppose that, as he worked on it, elaborating an imaginative vision marked in so many ways by its deliberate and radical unlikeness to the "real" world of his daily intercourse and ours, and achieved on a scale and with a thoroughness and meticulousness few before or since can have approached, he nonetheless did so with the claims of the one true creator of all things, visible and invisible, clearly in mind, and conscious that his own creative contribution, no matter how skillfully done, would finally "live" only if it in turn received the endorsement of Ilúvatar upon the ancient music: *Eä! Let these things Be!*

Chapter 5

TOLKIEN AND THE FUTURE
OF LITERARY STUDIES

David Lyle Jeffrey

Andrew Lang, the remarkable St. Andrews man for whom this series is named, was a literary historian as well as cultural polymath. As a literary historian, he had, as did Professor J. R. R. Tolkien in his justly famous Andrew Lang lecture here in 1939, a strong commitment to a greater inclusiveness in the canon. Succinctly, each desired a "recovery," for the sake of justice to the appreciation of the power of great literature, of those works, mostly older, which most transparently engage the supernatural. Many of these works, each believed, had been marginalized.

In Lang this desire for recovery took a number of forms, but we see its central character in the preface he wrote to his narrative about Joan of Arc, *The Maid of France* (1908). Lang was resisting the positivists and social realists in his learned audience when he wrote of the then uncomplimentary view of Joan's story and, by implication, others like it:

> . . . her memory was distasteful to all writers who disbelieved in her
> supernatural faculties, and in her inspiration. She had no business to
> possess faculties for which science could not account, and which common
> sense could not accept.[1]

Lang and Tolkien alike, it seems, thought the professionalized and pseudo-scientific study of literature in the twentieth century to be at severe risk of what amounted to an extreme scruple, a narrowness that might readily miss out altogether on the very reason story persists. It is precisely that character and function of literary expression which offers access to a tacit rather than explicit dimension of knowing that, they believed, makes the study of literature valuable. That this dimension is transparently also that of religion and the supernatural made the study of literature, on their view, a different order of *scientia*—but not at all, for that reason, either averse to science or a frivolous intellectual enterprise.

For Tolkien the order of knowing into which fairy tale gives access is proto-religious. Though *supernatural* he allows to be "a dangerous or difficult word in any of its senses,"[2] it is, precisely for that reason (as we are to see in such a work as *Sir Gawain and the Green Knight*), to be taken seriously.[3] It is essential, Tolkien insists, that the matter of faërie "be presented as 'true,'"[4] and that such works be appreciated for their "strong moral element . . . their inherent morality, not any allegorical *significatio*."[5] That the universe is *ipso facto* a moral ecology as well as a natural one is his consistent working assumption, no less evident in his philology and literary criticism than in his celebrated *The Lord of the Rings*.

On that account we can appreciate how, in his desire to rehabilitate fairy story, Tolkien is laboring to offset the *dour denouement*, the slide into depression so increasingly characteristic of late nineteenth-century and turn-of-the-century novels, especially the conventions of narrative in which realism tended to mandate the defeat of hope. When Tolkien further wishes to distinguish literature from drama—an otherwise perplexing passage in his lecture[6]—and in that context to say that the highest form of literature is the "Consolation of the Happy Ending,"[7] he is making the case for a literary category of hope. For his deeply Catholic, Christian worldview, *Commedia* is the truest form of the world's ultimate story, a story in which the deepest wellspring of desire is for redemption of that which has been lost, both to memory and to life. Against it, he says, is "Tragedy . . . the true form of Drama, the . . . opposite of Fairy story."[8]

If, however contrarily, you prefer drama, Tolkien says, you will recognize that it is "naturally hostile to Fantasy."[9] "You are [then] apt to misunderstand pure story-making," he says, and worse, apparently, "likely to prefer characters, even the basest and dullest, to things. Very little about trees as trees can be gotten into a play."[10] While one might wish in another context to debate Tolkien on this point (his revulsion from the scene with the witches in *Macbeth* rather widely misses, in my view, the real sources of horror and the supernatural in that play), we can see where he is going. The consummation of religion in his grand narrative is not catastrophe, as he so eloquently says, or *dyscatastrophe* but *eucatastrophe*—the "joy of deliverance," which "denies (in the face of much evidence . . .) universal final defeat, and in so far is *evangelium*."[11]

Yet let us consider, briefly, what Tolkien appears to have found alien in tragedy, "the true form of the drama."[12] Many literary critics, from Nietzsche to A. C. Bradley to George Steiner, have been formally of a similar opinion, but inclined to another slant, in which tragedy appears a more or less definitive insight into the human condition. On this view, of course, catastrophe really *must* predominate, the credible ending is disconsolate, grief annihilates joy, and hope is inevitably canceled by despair. But is it true, for all that, that tragedy provides a less useful—or dispensable—access to the supernatural?

The old Greek "goat song" (*tragedia*) was, of course, religion quint-essentially. Tragedy remained so, at least tacitly, from Sophocles and Aeschylus through to Marlowe and Shakespeare. Its *accessus* to the supernatural was gained not through joy but through horror. Yet the insights of tragedy into that which makes for character or virtue in men and women seem hardly less necessary to a full science of story than the disturbing supernaturalism of martyrs' tales and fairy story or fantasy.

Fantasy in particular has been, in some measure through the influence of Lang and Tolkien, at the beginning of the twenty-first century, remarkably rehabilitated. Classical and even Renaissance tragedy, on the other hand, like the heroic martyriological narrative of St. Joan, has been tending to dissipation in the contemporary curriculum, perhaps, we might suppose, for reasons analogous to those cited by Lang—their characteristic features run counter to modern science and are contrary to "common sense." Yet far more likely, I think, they diminish because they have depended, for comprehension, upon a *prior* literature of the supernatural, in terms of which their address to character, to virtue and vice, to spiritual agon and moral conflict alone make sense.

What I wish to suggest is that, without a credible literary engagement of those earlier works upon which tragedy (but not only tragedy) depends, we, a century later, may possibly lose this alternative category of great literature, and that this loss might in the end be more hostile to fantasy than Tolkien may have anticipated. Let me put my thesis in a slightly more angular way, and interrogatively: Is it not possible that the greatest threat to all serious literature is trivialization of the supernatural, whether in its joyous or its horrible aspect?

It recently happened that I was asked to review stage-script and offer, as promised a year earlier, an introductory lecture for our theatre company's production of *Doctor Faustus*. The script, when it arrived, proved rather forbidding. My colleague the director, in his effort to make Marlowe's sixteenth-century tragedy more accessible to twenty-first-century student and lay audiences, had interspersed (at lamentable cost to the original counterplot burlesque) excerpts from hellfire sermons of the eighteenth-century theologian and preacher Jonathan Edwards. To make the anachronism plausible, he had moved the venue from Wittenberg to Yale, and introduced, as fifth business and Professor Faustus's rector, Elisha Williams.

Now, howsoever much I strive to keep promises to my colleagues, I confess that I felt a certain doom settling upon me in this instance. In fact, my foreboding was such that I asked for my lecture to be scheduled the afternoon following (rather than, as at first planned, preceding) the opening night performance. Procrastination did not much help. Through the dim and strobe-lit chemical smoke the dashing young Mercutio-like Faustus zipped through his speeches like an eager telemarketer. Mephistophilis did not reappear as "an old Franciscan friar," despite the contention of Marlowe's Faustus that "that shape . . . befits a devil best,"[13] but instead as a rather voluptuous and extremely acrobatic young woman. In short, it was beginning to seem like the *pactum diaboli* theme a little too much resembled my own predicament.

Yet I tried to sympathize with the director and think through Marlowe's play with his contemporary problems in mind. Among them, I realized, he would have to anticipate that, even in the so-called Bible belt of America, the play's crucial biblical references would go mostly unrecognized. Two examples: when Faustus reads, "The reward of sin is death," he stops mid-sentence and concludes prematurely, "Ha! The reward of sin is death? That's hard."[14] Marlowe could count on his audience to know the rest of the verse. My colleague had to have his ex-machina Rector Williams fill it in from across the stage: "but the free gift of God is eternal life in Christ Jesus our Lord" (Rom 6:23). Similarly, when Faustus reads, "If we say that we have no sin, we deceive ourselves, and the truth is not in us," he cuts off the text to interpose a pre-emptive inference:

Why then belike we must sin,
And so consequently die.
Ay, we must die an everlasting death.
What doctrine call you this, che sera, sera,
What will be, shall be? Divinity adieu.[15]

My colleague had Williams then intone from his corner the balance of the interrupted verse: "If we confess our sins, He who is faithful and just will forgive us our sins and cleanse us from all unrighteousness" (1 John 1:9). Marlowe's point, evident to a biblically literate audience, was that scripture seemed "hard" to Faustus precisely because he closed his eyes to its fullness—i.e., because of his rejection of the "comfortable words" of the very same texts, the grace offered to reconcile our trans-gressions. It is of material interest that Faustus, for his own purposes, is from the outset interested only in half-truths.

But my colleague could not count on the audience to fill in either the rhetorical or the theological blanks. In the contemporary Church of the Blessed Overhead Projector, biblical literacy lags well behind that of the Elizabethan theater. I thought for a while that might be the worst of my problem—but soon recognized that in thinking so, I had undershot the mark. Nowhere in the play, despite a host of spectacular special effects he could not have imagined at all, was there evoked anything like the sheer horror of hell necessary to constitute the devil's pact for our audi-ence as the stuff of "tragedy," or to render the final long death speech of Faustus even plausibly terrifying.

So that is what I made my talk about: the Renaissance fear of hell and damnation. To culminate, since I was lecturing in the theater, and from the set itself, I acted out the last long speech, aided by the presence and taunting last words of both Good and Bad Angel. My effort was followed by a burst of (to me) uncomfortably enthusiastic applause. (Some people are apparently pleased to see an old professor damned to hell; to see it happen to a provost apparently excites near universal glee.)

It strikes me that it is quite difficult to get students in the twenty-first century to take hell seriously. Its most familiar guise—that imprecation which makes "hell" a direct object of the verb "to go," usually offered as a categorical imperative in the second person—hardly now even counts as a real curse. It just encourages the telemarketer to call on someone else, perhaps a colloquial vindication of Jean-Paul Sartre's unduly famous remark that "Hell is other people."[16]

But is this a hellish enough hell to make sense of *The Tragicall Historie of Doctor Faustus*, or Dante's *Inferno*, Milton's *Paradise Lost*, or even Charles Williams's *Descent into Hell*, let alone the teachings of Jesus? The thoughtful reader may have serious doubts. And worse still, without some sense of awe in respect of divine *holiness*, how are students to conjure with the agonized impatience of the reply Mephistophilis makes to Faustus's literalistic question, "How comes it then that thou art out of hell?"

> Meph. Why this *is* hell, nor am I out of it.
> Thinkst thou that I who saw the face of God,
> And tasted the eternal joys of heaven,
> Am not tormented with ten thousand hells,
> In being depriv'd of everlasting bliss?[17]

Who now can feel the inconsolable ache in these devilish lines?

It is a commonplace among those of us who teach literature that some of the world's greatest texts are, by now, extremely difficult to teach to undergraduates. While the reasons vary from text to text—premodern, early modern, modern—the reasons offered usually implicate our students' lack of linguistic amplitude or want of literary foundations as a context for approaching the works in question. There has been a certain amount of pious and quite futile hand wringing about this and, much more commonly, emphatic curricular exclusion of what is seen as a culturally estranged literature.

Conceivably, I think, preservation of some great vernacular works—and not only of dramatic art—may now come to depend upon scholars who are representative of subcultural communities, those whose call to learning comes in the context of a personal religious formation. But to accomplish this purpose, even they will have to do what all scholars do who would preserve a great but unfashionable literature, whether for their own purposes or the common good of humanity. They will have first to read and teach with deep understanding the foundational literatures among which the subsequent great works hold their own conversation. Not even teachers in confessional colleges can count on the churches or departments of religion to have done this accountably.

We readily accept this sort of intertextual necessity for literature composed in other, nonbiblical religious contexts. Hence, the continuing pertinence of certain observations of Voltaire, indicating the crucial role of foundational books for everything else in the literary cultures he identifies:

> The whole of Africa, right to Ethiopia, and Nigritia obeys the book of the Alcoran, after having staggered under the book of the Gospel. China is ruled by the moral book of Confucius; a greater part of India by the book of the Veda. Persia was governed for centuries by one of the books of the Zarathustras.[18]

For teaching postcolonial or world literature, few would argue with Voltaire. Yet in our guild, we have had an extreme scruple where the "book of the Gospel" and Western literature is concerned. Notably, professional aversion to our own traditional "governing" book is proving to be coincident to an ongoing crisis of coherence for our profession—a discipline, of course, far younger than classics or any of the other core disciplines mastered and then rejected by Marlowe's Faustus.

It is notably the case that English literature became a university discipline only in the nineteenth century, and at least in part as a rejection of both classical and religious foundations. The genealogy is instructive. Though Headmaster Thomas Arnold of Rugby remains almost as memorable for the power of his proclamation of traditional Christian verities as for his famous graduates, most of these more famous students—like Arthur Clough and his own son Matthew—soon departed from the senior Arnold's religious belief in order to embrace an ideal of culture from which the living faith had been largely excised. The first professor of poetry at Oxford to lecture in English rather than Latin, Arnold signaled the future of the discipline not only by focusing on *The Modern Element in Literature* but by turning literary education itself toward social construction and explicitly away from biblical revelation. Yet in his revolutionary wish for the study of literature to provide an alternate clerisy and to preserve reading of the Bible not for religious but for literary purposes, he exhibited an unstable tension that has bedeviled literary formation in our guild ever since.

Justification for the place of vernacular literary studies in the university depends upon a commitment to teach more than simply rudimentary skills on an order that, for the most part, would not once have obtained a passing grade at Rugby. Our university prominence has depended still more upon successfully ascribing high and (let us confess it) quasi-religious ideals to an increasingly low and secular reading practice. The advertised function of the practitioner is to make culture itself more widely available (in Arnold one moves from reading Homer in the original to comparing English translations of Homer), but by doing so ostensibly in search of a "grand style" expressive of a certain "nobility of the human spirit." If the poet "sees life steadily and sees it whole," the well-read critic all the more so. As poetry assumed the functions of religion among Arnold's successors, at least down to the New Critics and Northrop Frye, there was plenty of high-sounding stuff for its professors to sell to college administrators, regents, and many students. Arnold's "perfecting of a national right reason" worked in nicely with the later "pooled social intelligence" of John Dewey as well as with numerous other identifications of salvation with the state and of virtue with a never-to-be-ended quest for poetic—hence conveniently subjective—truth.

As we look over our shoulder, then, we can see how contention that the classics are "the noblest recorded thoughts of man," the "only oracles which are not decayed"[19] reflects an archaic secular piety that did not long persist after the founding of our discipline. Nor was this reverence ever so fully extended in the modern university to biblical literature. For Arnold, enamored of Goethe and the Romantics, traditional religion is already bankrupt and, as in one of his more famous dismissals he puts it: "the strongest part of our religion to-day is its unconscious poetry."[20] Conscious poetry, especially of the Romantics, he reckoned to possess a "higher truth and a higher seriousness."[21] James Joyce simply echoes Arnold when Stephen, in *Portrait of the Artist as a Young Man*, refers to literature as "the highest and most spiritual art."[22]

As all here know, these sentiments continued to be the prevailing secular pieties of our guild in the early 1960s in America. By the 1980s they too had been, of course, irrevocably interrogated, shaken down, and in some considerable measure dissolved. But the new revolutionaries were more than gradual secularists; among them a more candid apostasy was a requirement of the license to practice. They were thoroughgoing iconoclasts, and not in any sentimental sense worshippers. Their revolution has pretty effectively "done in" Arnold, and we might now suspect, most of the apostolic succession of his clerisy with him.

In much of the English-speaking world, the formal study of literature is in disarray. Even when English departments focus on books of the most slender claim to nobility of thought, let alone grandness of style, pressing rather for what is taken to be more marketable fashion and relevance, students have continued to disperse to majors in communication studies, media-telecommunications, journalism, technical writing, cinema criticism, and cultural studies. Meanwhile, our discipline has acquired a popular notoriety for being the purveyor not of high and noble verities but of low and often trivial advocacies. Consequently, as the late Bernard Williams observed, even the primary literature itself has suffered from "some very reductive criticisms of traditional academic authority":

> If the canon of works or writers or philosophies to be studied, and the methods of interpreting them, and the historical narratives that explain those things, are all equally and simultaneously denounced as ideological impositions, we are indeed left with a space structured only by power.[23]

But such diminishment is hardly confined to the canonical status of texts (as deans of humanities and provosts will attest). The loss of literary authority to an utterly reductive account, as Williams further observes, deprives the critics themselves of sufficient power to sustain their enterprise. Both Lang and Tolkien were surely right to anticipate that much. Put more crudely: the status of literary study as an apprenticeship to wisdom had the advantage of appearing even to the unwise (e.g., administrators) as a species of learning probably deserving of some environmental protection; current rationalizations for literary study as a venue for avant-garde politics, competitive with the therapeutic social sciences, quickly lose traction.

Authority, notably, accrues to possession of—or capacity for—truth of the high order that readers from Aristotle to Wordsworth (in the *Preface*) to Nietzsche ("poetry aims to be . . . the unvarnished expression of the truth"[24]) have associated with the books most worth reading. Whereas our modern discipline began with Arnold in the credo that religious truths had been, in literature, supplemented by the "higher truths" of nature;[25] we may well have approached a survival limit for our guild with postmodernist assertions that literature affords us no stable or shareable truths at all. In his provocative book *Truth and Truthfulness*, philosopher Williams argues for a profound reversal of what he calls the "deconstructive vortex":

> If the passion for truthfulness is merely controlled and stilled without being satisfied, it will kill the activities it is supposed to support. This may be one of the reasons why, at the present time, the study of the humanities runs a risk of sliding from professional seriousness, through professionalization, to a finally disenchanted careerism.[26]

The drift of Williams's argument is actually toward a reassertion of that uncommon sense we still call "common," of a revaluing of pre-reflective openness to truth in relation to language, even of a sort of "primitive trust"[27] in such "virtues of truth" as "accuracy and sincerity," and the "pooling of information" as a common good.[28] There is more than a touch of Arnold here, but also a pointing to the need for something more substantial.

Williams's reflections correspond to my own in querying claims, albeit now enshrined as critical dogma, that there are no longer sustaining common stories, or grand narratives.[29] Tolkien's trilogy has become in itself a refutation of such claims. If we are thinking about the dissolution of modern European socialist agendas there is, of course, a certain rhetorical *apropos* to this claim; if we are thinking of, say, African literature it makes almost no sense at all. Among writers in China, whose formal Marxist grand narrative has also stuttered to a stop, many contemporary novelists have identified openly with religious story, particularly the Christian grand narrative. (Among the most prominent Christian novelists are Lao She, Xu Dishan, Bing Xing, and Mu Dan.) There is even a new literary style called "biblical" (*sheng jing ti*), whose characteristics are described as "objective, truthful, terse."[30]

However oddly for us, it is in parts of Africa, Asia, and South America that our own greatest older texts are now perhaps most carefully taught and intertextually reflected. But I wonder if the pendulum may not yet swing about here too, if only because our employment cannot much longer be sustained by the purveying of trendy ephemerality alone. To return to Williams, for us too

> [t]he need to make sense of the past reasserts itself. It is particularly so when the smooth order of things is disturbed by violence, if only to answer the questions "Why?" "Why us?" "Where from?" Communitarian politics (and, at the limit, renewed tribal wars) are one area in which the need is very much alive, and it appears, too, in the interest in current historical disputes. . . . The demand for an explicit and definite story about one's own people or nation is only one form of it, and that particular demand has been more urgent in some places than in others.[31]

Tolkien, it seems to me, might credibly be described as having made an attempt, through recovery of faërie, to respond to that urgent need. But he is hardly to be blamed if his work was not, at least for the future hope for literary studies, in itself sufficient to provide a contemporary foundation.

The present crisis for literary study has been long in the making—effectively, it is the outworking, I believe, of a congenital defect. For

others it has been more attractive to think of it as merely an acciden-
tal disorder, the etiology of which has been examined, belatedly, and
with eloquent alarm by critics such as George Steiner since the 1960s
and Terry Eagleton, beginning in the 1980s. In his essay, "To Civilize
our Gentlemen," Steiner's nominal occasion was arcane, doctoral dis-
sertations and thin, literary journalism; but his underlying targets were
the failed "rational and moral optimism" of I. A. Richards and Henry
Sidgwick, which rightly he identifies as secondhand Arnold, and the aes-
theticism, however elegant, of F. R. Leavis and Arthur Quiller Couch.
Steiner's gesture toward medicine for the ailing discipline, however
much I affirm his notion of a multilingual *cortesia*, is by itself inadequate.
Steiner asks: "Is it not as important for the survival of feeling today . . .
to know another living language as it was once important for a man to
be intimate with the classics and Scripture?"[32] To this I would answer
"no"—that these sources of common understanding are not equivalent in
value. A secondary good cannot long be sustained without the primary
good from which it proceeds. For love of the neighbor to be sustained, at
least on the biblical view, it must grow out of love for God with all our
heart, soul, and mind (Matt 22:37-40). From this prior love, neighbor
love obtains its true value, coherence, and credible modes of expression
in whatever language lies mutually to hand.

For Terry Eagleton, a post-Catholic Marxist for whom the authority of his new religion lay precisely in its ethical rather than aesthetic
claims, it was the failure of literary study following the 1960s to keep
in the vanguard of socialist reform that occasioned his greatest anxiet-
ies; the "crisis" he addressed (1983) was likewise a crisis of coherence.
For Eagleton the turn from literature to cultural theory has since then
degenerated further into a socially acceptable yet entirely narcissistic
self-preoccupation in which "quietly-spoken middle class students hud-
dle diligently in libraries, at work on sensationalist subjects like vam-
pirism and eye-gouging, cyborgs and porno movies."[33] His wrath rises
proportionately to his sense that professional literary study has fled from
public and political purpose to radically anarchic self-absorption: "The
emancipation which has failed in the streets and factories" he writes in
After Theory, "could be acted out instead in erotic intensities or the float-

ing signifier."[34] Yes. But is such an overdetermined diagnosis enough to chart a way out of our present malaise?

Steiner and Eagleton are types, respectively, of Kierkegaard's "aesthetic" and "ethical" man. Each laments but also remains locked into the Arnoldian legacy, despite ardent attempts to rise above it. We should empathize, but with a more self-examining circumspection. Steiner admits, correctly, that while "'Art for art' is a tactical slogan . . . pressed to its logical consequences it is pure narcissism."[35] Eagleton, while he recognizes the tactical advantage for radical social reform in coded discourse, is as appalled as Steiner at the loss of elegance and clarity in the wake of postmodern psychobabble. Each staggers under the professional burden of a discourse without rankable values, the Babel-effect of a secular religion gone wrong on both truth and beauty, and whose acolytes, cheerless in their alternate fits of denial and despair, discourse incommensurably even with each other, let alone with an increasingly indifferent world. It is not surprising, on these accounts, that some of us are losing quorum in the classroom.

The parallels with the near-modern history of institutional religion, in particular Christianity, are many—too many to explore here. The loss of any authority sufficiently transcendent to command a common allegiance and thus create a common discourse is but one of these parallels. It is no merely secular reflex, I think, that Steiner is made unhappy by that apparent permissiveness in the guild whereby "[w]e can say any truth and any falsehood"[36] and get away with it; nor is it extrinsic to his radical left social purpose that Eagleton, in his latest book, defends the idea of absolute truth and objectivity as fervently, if not as cogently, as does Bernard Williams.[37]

Since at least the time of Aristotle, who asserted in his *Poetics* that fiction has about it an order of truth more universal than history, the hope for shareable truth has been an indispensable sustainer for the social authority of literature.[38] One came to the theater at Athens because the truths made flesh on the stage were more than transient truths. This gave even to a dramatized *denial* of truth a terrible power to wound and heal. But just as with the religious plays of Aeschylus and Sophocles, Shakespeare and Marlowe, so for all literature that, in the end, bids to be taken seriously by the wider community of thoughtful minds: at bottom, the only guarantor of communal truth is transcendent truth; the only guarantor of authority is the near presence of an ultimate and abiding authority.

"If no authority, then only power."[39] Yet the power we in our discipline have wrested from authority is proving to be a rather feeble order of power; just how feeble, perhaps especially in straitened economic circumstances, the next decade will likely tell more completely. Put positively, it seems to me that the best hope for literature as a secular discipline is for it to reacquire its access to some sort of moral and rhetorical authority; the rush to trade such authority for power has proved to be a very bad bargain indeed.

In communities of those who yet think that truth has consequences—in time and out of it—there is accordingly, however, an added obligation of neighbor love: to teach the Greats and to do so in a fashion richly affirmative of their relation to founding religious texts. An advantage to readers whose common treasure is the common Book, and for whom common prayer and a common sense that salvation is both desirable and not a purely individual matter, is that they can become confident enough in their own identity to take the ultimate concerns of others, past and present, a little more seriously. They should be able—if they have not entirely forgotten their calling—to give to our older literature an intellectually responsible treatment of its primary religious and moral as well as stylistic dimensions, even, or perhaps especially, when the ending confronts us with horror and catastrophe.

Matthew Arnold thought that the spiritual capital of Christianity would readily transmute at comparably high value to secular cultural capital, the prestige of its canons carrying over into a secular clerisy of the literate. Accordingly, he was happy for the grandiloquence of the King James Bible and Book of Common Prayer to persist as some guerdon of their authority, and even to echo in the prose of literary scholars. But after one hundred and fifty years all that capital has been pretty much spent. Arnold and his successors, I believe, were simply wrong to think we could keep even these stylistic virtues without the high order of spiritual reverence to which they were attached.

Faustus, we may remember, was willing to go from half-truths through illusions about his own power to a kind of rabid incoherence in which he proved at last to have no power at all. Having rejected the undergirding fullness of the common Book, believing himself superior to it in knowledge, wisdom, and mastery, he took up instead certain books of magic and necromancy, by which in his search for self-aggrandizement he anathematized to himself the "New Testament and the Hebrew Psalter." In the end, in that last horrible scene, as the clock strikes and the demons draw nigh, he cries out in vain, "I'll burn my books!"[40] His attempt at reformation, however, came all too late. What the Renaissance audience could see (can a modern audience perceive this?) was that what he probably needed to do, at the very outset, was to tell "German Cornelius and Valdes," most emphatically, where to go.

Now it must be admitted that in literature, hell is more full of notable academics, perhaps, than we should like. Among memorable examples, Dante's Brunetto Latini, for his reasons, Williams's Professor Wentworth for his. What these denizens have in common is a lifelong practice of retreat from the common good, and of its concomitant, rationalizing away any sense of accountability to the truth of the other. Perseverant egoism and almost absurd levels of narcissism are, in each case, made possible by a disdaining refusal of self-transcendent, mind-independent reality. Particular rationalizations for this or that denial are often, of course, ingenious: what gives each catastrophic fall its tragic dimension is audience appreciation that "rationalization is the homage paid by sin to guilty knowledge."[41] The literate audience knows it was a choice.

Coherence depends upon a common sense, a sense of objective value to which, communally, we may appeal. Language itself will not otherwise work. As Williams observes, "Children learn language in many ways and in many different kinds of situation, but one essential way is that they hear sentences being used in situations in which those sentences are plainly true."[42] In this respect also, "[e]xcept ye . . . become as little children, ye shall not enter into the kingdom of heaven" (Matt 18:3; KJV).

Can we bear the burden of obligatory clarity, even to preserve our livelihood, let alone the common good (the "commune profit" as Gower called it) of our students and neighbors? It may not seem obvious to many of us just how easy it is to make a pact with the devil, then all too belatedly to regret it. Perhaps too few of us in this business now believe we have a soul to lose. Yet, for our discipline, there surely is a soul to lose. What I want to suggest today is that for some of us who profess literature at least, "if sin by custom grow not into nature,"[43] as Marlowe's Erasmian old man has it, it may not be too late to revive our options. Tragedy serves as a warning.

Tolkien favored the recovery of faërie at least in part because he was intent upon the happy ending, the potential of literature for consolation. His dislike of the drama is focused on tragedy because in it the very form of closure depends upon a realized catastrophe. One wonders how eucatastrophic plays such as Shakespeare's *Winter's Tale* or *Pericles* might have been integrated into his thinking about the worth of drama as a genre. It seems to me improbable that recovery of the religious power of great literature can be complete without an acceptance of the complementary necessity of unhappy endings, Dame Julian of Norwich and T. S. Eliot's oft remembered citation of her notwithstanding. In Christian theological terms, the assurance that "all shall be well" does not mean that all shall be happy, any more that the proposition "God is good" requires as its equivalent, "just the way we'd like him."

Let me be clear. I am inclined to consent with Jacques Maritain (against Arnold) that "it is a deadly error to expect poetry to produce the supersubstantial nourishment of man."[44] That higher, more noble nourishment lies with the Greater Book. At the same time I also believe in the power of literature to enable our will to truth. I am convinced, however, that without intellectually accountable access to a full range of texts that encounter and explore the supernatural—even in its horrible aspects—very many lesser, yet still very great, expressions of truth may go without understanding, and eventually even unread and unreprinted, like unto the beasts which perish. That would be for far more than ourselves a tragedy; it might also, and perhaps irredeemably, further diminish the residual authority of our fragile discipline.

Chapter Six

TOLKIEN AND THE SURRENDERING OF POWER

Loren Wilkinson

I have been asked to say some things comparing Tolkien's *The Lord of the Rings* story with Peter Jackson's *Lord of the Rings* film. Perhaps, in view of last week's eleven Oscars, I also need to say a word about my title.[1] Let me stress that I am speaking of a failure *in* the films, not the failure *of* the films. Obviously they are spectacular successes. Considered as films, I think they are very great movies indeed, far better than we deserve. Nevertheless, when they are examined against the backdrop of Tolkien's written story, almost everyone, including the filmmakers, will acknowledge certain necessary shortcomings. To speak of these is a daunting task, since all who know both books and films have their favorite list of unforgivable omissions and intrusions, and are eager to share it. I have a list like that myself, but I would like to place it in a context that, I hope, will allow this comparison of two uniquely important cultural achievements to show us something about the very nature of story—particularly the hero story that is the ancient backbone of literature, and of which Tolkien's *The Lord of the Rings* provides a particularly good example.

But first I want to deal with a frequent objection to the films: that is the assumption that Tolkien himself would have been deeply opposed to the very concept of making a movie of this story. We can lay that fear quickly to rest. The principal evidence is a letter written by Tolkien to Christopher and Faith Tolkien in September 1957, shortly after a London taxi drew up in front of his house in Oxford

> . . . filling 76 Stanfield with strange men and stranger women—I thought the taxi would never stop disgorging. But this Mr. Ackerman brought some really astonishingly good pictures (Rackham rather than Disney) and some remarkable color photographs. They have apparently toured America shooting mountain and desert scenes that seem to fit the story. The story Line or Scenario was, however, on a lower level. In fact bad. But it looks as if business might be done. Stanley U. and I have agreed on our policy: *Art or Cash.* Either very profitable terms indeed; or absolute author's veto on objectionable features or alterations.[2]

It is clear from this letter that Tolkien was not at all against the idea of a film—even an animated version, as this was—and that he would have accepted pretty serious compromises with the story if the price were high enough. (British academics then, as now, were notoriously underpaid, and the enormous financial success of the book was still in the future. Tolkien also felt an obligation to his publisher, who had taken a risk with the book, to return some profit).

Further evidence of the seriousness with which Tolkien took this film proposal can be found in the detailed comments Tolkien made on the proposed storyline. (Humphrey Carpenter includes an eight-page excerpt of these in the collected *Letters.*) Tolkien begins by taking the project very seriously, and the comparisons of his comments here with the completed Jackson film make for a very interesting study. At one point, for example, objecting to the proposed portrayal of Goldberry in the Tom Bombadil scene (one of the most lamented omissions from the recent film), Tolkien says, "she had far better disappear than make a meaningless appearance."[3] The comment suggests Tolkien's willingness to accept serious cuts. His patience runs thin and gives out by the end, however, when he concludes that the treatment of the final part is "totally unacceptable to me, as a whole and in detail. . . . *The Lord of the Rings* cannot be garbled like that."[4] Nevertheless, the nature of his comments show that he was not at all opposed to the *idea* of making a movie of his book. So a study of Tolkien's early commentary on the storyline of a film that was never made suggests pretty clearly not only that Tolkien would have given his permission for the film but would have been generally pleased with Jackson's adaptation (though certainly not at every point: "Too many battles, not enough walking, too much magic, not enough attention to the seasons"—these are recurring grumbles by Tolkien, and they could be made of the Jackson films as well, excellent as they are). But Tolkien did not reject the film medium as a worthy means of telling a story. Story is story. As he put it in his letter of criticism on the proposed film's storyline:

> The canons of narrative art in any medium cannot be wholly different: and the failure of poor films is often precisely in exaggeration, and in the intrusion of unwarranted matter owing to not perceiving where the core of the original lies.[5]

I would like to argue that even this very successful trilogy of films contains such a failure to perceive "where the core of the original lies." And perhaps, I want to suggest, it is a necessary failure. For to a very unusual degree in heroic stories, the core of this story, though supremely life-affirming, is not *heroic* in any sense that film can convey to audiences whose sensibility has been shaped by the more typical hero story. Films that are to have wide audience appeal today seem to require a different sort of hero than the ones we find in the story Tolkien wrote.

The Tolkien films succeed very well with that traditional hero story. But there is another aspect of "story" that is very difficult—perhaps impossible—for the film medium to portray adequately. It is the story not of the warrior or the wanderer, but of to and for what they come home. It is the story of the gardener, the homemaker, and it is exceptionally difficult to make vivid in a movie. The great strength of Tolkien's book is that it regularly balances (and to some degree *subverts*) the hero story with the gardener story, and this the films fail—perhaps necessarily—to do.

Here I need to take a step back and reflect a bit on a useful theory about the basic shape of story. It has been outlined popularly by Joseph Campbell in works like *The Hero with a Thousand Faces*. A much more exhaustive treatment of the same idea forms the core of Northrop Frye's work, especially *The Anatomy of Criticism*, and his later works on the Bible such as *The Great Code*. The basic story, says this theory, can be described as a journey in which a hero, usually reluctantly, in voluntary or involuntary exile from his (rarely her) homeland, sets out to accomplish a task. After overcoming many obstacles and vanquishing many enemies, and passing through a kind of death in life often symbolized as an underground journey, the hero returns against all odds from the kingdom of death to his homeland, usually wedding a bride in the process. Frye argues further that this journey provides us with a kind of anatomy of types of literature: the idyllic existence in the homeland is the subject matter of romance; the exclusion, wandering, and death of the hero, the matter of tragedy; the life-in-death underground journey, the subject of irony (where, he says, much modern fiction lies); and the resurrection, wedding, and triumphant return, the stuff of comedy. Thus tragedies end in funerals, and comedies end in weddings, fertility, or babies. There is often a seasonal complement to this story. Romance is associated with summer, tragedy with autumn, irony with winter, and comedy with spring.

There is obviously a great deal of power in this sort of analysis, and I have used it often myself in teaching literature—especially the relationship of literature to the Christian story, which this story-shape resembles. And *The Lord of the Rings* follows this pattern very closely, alluding rather pointedly to the Christian year as well, since the Fellowship of the Ring sets out from Rivendell on December 25, and the Ring is destroyed just after the first full moon after the vernal equinox, the date of Easter.

But like most patterns, this one simplifies the nature of stories. A little reflection shows that in half of these four types of story—the tragic and the comic—there is more action and movement than in the other half (romance and irony). Life in the summer kingdom of romance and the winter discontent of irony is more even-keeled: joyous in the one, perhaps dully painful in the other. But until they tip over, or up, into tragedy or comedy, it is pretty much one day after another.

In fact, this common schemata for understanding story combines in one kind of story, that of the hero (who is usually also a warrior, and traditionally a male) with another sort of story, the story of the *gardener*. The real hero of the Tolkien story, as many have pointed out, is not

Aragorn the king, or Gandalf the wizard, or any of the sword-bearing warriors. It is not even Frodo the Ring-bearer; it is rather Sam the gardener. The hero-warrior is by necessity a pilgrim, a wanderer: he is on his way somewhere else, on a quest or a campaign. Battle is a necessary part of his story. The gardener is a stay-at-home. He (or more often she) puts down roots: either (to follow Frye's typology) in the idyllic summer of the homeland, or in the difficult winter of exile. There's nothing particularly spectacular or cinematic about the tasks of the gardener—or, to use a loaded word that characterizes Sam perfectly, of the homemaker. Those tasks are characterized mainly by patience, care, and love—and in Sam's case, by a heavy pack that contains, among other things, cooking pots, and hence a semblance of domesticity and home.

The contrast between these two sorts of story is put brilliantly in an essay by the American novelist Ursula Le Guin. Le Guin may well be judged the twentieth century's greatest writer of fantasy after Tolkien (in part because, as she herself acknowledges, she wrote the best of it, the first three *Earthsea* books, before she fell under the spell of Tolkien, whom she admires tremendously and whose influence, she says, she might not have been able to resist).

In a frankly feminist essay called "The Carrier Bag Theory of Fiction" (what she intends by the title will become obvious) Le Guin speculates on what we know about the prehistoric environment in which humans became storytellers. In that environment, she argues, we know that people obtained most of their protein from gathering "seeds, roots sprouts, shoots, leaves, nuts, berries, fruits, and grains. . . ." It was, normally, a pretty easy life: "The average prehistoric person could make a nice living in about a fifteen-hour work week"[6]—leaving lots of spare time. In that spare time, says Le Guin,

> . . . maybe the restless ones who didn't have a baby around to enliven their life, or skill in making or cooking or singing, or very interesting thoughts to think, decided to slope off and hunt mammoths. The skillful hunters then would come staggering back with a load of meat, a lot of ivory, and a story. It wasn't the meat that made the difference. It was the story.[7]

Thus, argues Le Guin, early in the history of story, hero tales of adventure and conquest overshadowed the more ordinary and life-affirming tales of growing things, gardens, and home. For, says Le Guin,

> [i]t is hard to tell a really gripping tale of how I wrested a wild-oat seed from its husk, and then another, and then another, and then another, and then another, and then I scratched my gnat bites . . . and then I found another patch of oats. . . . No it does not compare, it cannot compete with how I thrust my spear deep into the titanic hairy flank while Oob, impaled on one huge sweeping tusk, writhed screaming, and blood spouted everywhere in crimson torrents, and Boob was crushed to jelly when the mammoth fell on him as I shot my unerring arrow straight though eye to brain.

> That story not only has Action, it has a Hero. Heroes are powerful. Before you know it, the men and women in the wild-oat patch and their kids and the skills of the makers and the thoughts of the thoughtful and the songs of the singers are all part of it, have all been pressed into service in the tale of the Hero. But it isn't their story. It's his.[8]

Heroes make the most compelling stories. They also make the most compelling movies. But in terms of Northrop Frye's four-part division of literature, they really are at home only in half of the pattern; in fact, almost by definition, heroes are not at home at all: they are always going somewhere else, moving on, whether to exile and death (in tragedy) or restoration and return (as in comedy). And movies (look at the word) are best suited for showing *movement*. One of the most damning comments one can make of a film is that it "doesn't go anywhere." But there is, I repeat, another part of story which is about staying put, about being at home—either in a good place, as in romance, or a bad place, as in the various ironic winters of our discontent. It is the great genius of Tolkien's narrative to hold the hero-story and the home-story in a wonderful dynamic tension that the film fails, perhaps inevitably, to reproduce. Sam, in a memorable conversation on the nature of story on the stairs of Cirith Ungol reflects on the ultimately empty life of the homeless hero:

We hear about those that just went on—and not all to a good end, mind you; at least not to what folks inside a story and not outside it call a good end—you know, coming home, and finding things all right, though not quite the same. . . . But those aren't always the best tales to hear, though they may be the best tales to get landed in! I wonder what sort of tale we've fallen into.[9]

"Not always the best tales to hear"—nor, we might add, the best tales to make a movie of. In the same scene Sam describes the *point* of the stories where homes and gardens are given their rightful place: "Plain ordinary rest and sleep, and waking up to a morning's work in the garden. I'm afraid that's all I'm hoping for all the time." But it doesn't make much of a movie.

Le Guin describes this type of fiction which explores daily life in contrast with the hero story. She begins with a famous hero scene from another epic film, *2001: A Space Odyssey:*

Where is that wonderful, big, long, hard thing, a bone, I believe, that the Ape Man first bashed somebody with in the movie and then, grunting with ecstasy at having achieved the first proper murder, flung up into the sky, and whirling there it became a space ship thrusting its way into the cosmos to fertilize it and produce at the end of the movie a lovely fetus, a boy of course, drifting around the Milky Way without (oddly enough) any womb, any matrix at all? I don't know. I don't even care. I'm not telling that story. We've heard it, we've all heard all about all the sticks and spears and swords, the things to bash and poke and hit with, the long, hard things, but we have not heard about the thing to put things in, the container for the thing contained. That is a new story. That is news . . . with or before the tool that forces energy outward, we made the tool that brings energy home.[10]

In this context Le Guin proposes "the Carrier Bag theory of story": "It is a human thing to do to put something you want, because it's useful, edible, or beautiful, into a bag, or a basket, or a bit of rolled bark or leaf . . . and then take it home with you, home being another, larger kind of pouch or bag."[11]

The novel, says Le Guin, is this kind of "fundamentally unheroic" story. "The natural, proper, fitting shape of the novel might be that of a sack, a bag. A book holds words. Words hold things. They bear meanings. A novel is a medicine bundle, holding things in a particular, powerful relation to one another and to us."[12] This is not a particularly cinematic genre but it describes an important aspect of *The Lord of the Rings*. Whatever else it is, it is a *collection* of things: songs, histories, places, names (the carrier bag nature of the story is most obvious in the wonderful miscellanies of the appendix). Many of these diverse things (like the autumnal loveliness of Tom Bombadil and Goldberry) can only impede the forward motion of the story. So the hero-driven film must leave them out. What Le Guin says about the tendency of the hero story to take over the carrier bag story is even more true in film:

> [T]he Hero has frequently taken [the novel] over, that being his imperial nature and uncontrollable impulse, to take everything over and run it while making stern decrees and laws to control his uncontrollable impulse to kill it. . . . [F]irst, that the proper shape of the narrative should be that of the arrow or spear, starting *here* and going straight *there* . . . second, that the central concern of narrative, including the novel, is conflict, and third, that the story isn't any good if [the hero] isn't in it.[13]

Here, it seems to me that Le Guin (speaking in reaction) has overstated the case. Tolkien's story leaves no doubt that there is a necessary place in story for pilgrimage, quest, battle, heroes: but such things are empty without homes and gardens to return to—a fact never forgotten in the story but sadly overlooked in the film.

Now let me conclude by looking a bit more specifically at the film and the story through the lens provided by this understanding of two kinds of story: the hero story and garden story. It seems pretty clear that, with a few exceptions, the pressure of the hero story has eclipsed the garden story. There are some exceptions. Great and loving care was exercised in showing the domesticity of the Shire and its fruits and flowers. Surely this is one of the high points of the film, establishing very well the fertile summer-land the hobbits must leave, and to which they return in the end. These opening and closing scenes are perfectly in keeping with Tolkien's purpose, down to the concluding words in both book and film, "Well, I'm back."

Yet this is almost all we see of the themes of home and garden. With the exception of these framing glimpses, the film lets the swords, battles, and travels crowd out the many small but significant glimpses of rest, rootedness, and stewardship. Let me list some of the more obvious ones.

I have already mentioned the most obvious: the complete exclusion of the three chapters—nearly forty pages—that refer to Tom Bombadil. While agreeing that this is, in terms of forward-moving storyline, the most expendable part of the whole trilogy, its loss is typical—and in terms of Le Guin's analysis, highly significant. Whatever we make of the curious relationship of Tom and Goldberry, it is clear that they live in an ancient, unchanging relationship with their place. Tom is "at home" here more profoundly than anyone else in the whole story: and he has been here from the beginning. Like Beorn in *The Hobbit*, whom he resembles somewhat, Tom is a beekeeper, and the place flows with both milk and honey. Beans ripen in the September rain. He is helpful to the travelers, but their tasks and quests are not his. Significantly, he is the only character in the story who is completely indifferent to the Ring, and on whom it exerts no influence. (The Ring does not make him invisible, but he can make the Ring vanish, much to Frodo's consternation.) Inexplicable in terms of normal hero stories, the Bombadil interlude, like the Shire, provides a kind of center for the other part of story: the story of people who are deeply rooted in their place. Understandable as its exclusion is, its absence nevertheless subtly skews the whole story.

A similar but less obvious exclusion occurs in the second film when we get to the much larger southern equivalent of the Old Forest, Fanghorn. Here too there are keepers, this time of the trees. Treebeard is clearly a kind of shepherd of the trees, yet this stewardly relationship of ents to trees is passed over in the film. The ents are mainly significant as warriors, not tree-shepherds. Most notably, there is little sign or mention in the films of "the entwives," who are almost perfect embodiments of the other aspect of story—that of the unheroic gardener. (The "extended" version of the film contains *brief* allusion to the entwives.) The ents are wanderers; the entwives are gardeners. As Treebeard tells the story:

But the Entwives gave their mind to the lesser trees, and to the meads in the sunshine beyond the feet of the forests; and they saw the sloe in the thicket, and the wild apple and the cherry blossoming in spring, and the green herbs in the waterlands in summer, and the seeding grasses in the autumn fields. . . . So the Entwives made gardens to live in. But we Ents went on wandering, and we only came to the gardens now and again.[14]

Eventually the entwives disappear from all but the memories and songs of the ents. But they hardly appear at all in the film, and the ents are reduced to warrior trees. Again, the absence is probably necessary: how does one film a memory? But like Bombadil, the entwives are a crucial counterweight to the wandering and fighting of the rest of the hero story.

One more brief but significant omission: one of the more grievous liberties the filmmakers took with Tolkien's text was turning Faramir into a power-hungry kidnapper and moving much of the hobbits' interaction with him to a battle in Osgiliath (where, in the book, no hobbit goes) from the place Tolkien describes as "Ithilien, the garden of Gondor," even in desolation keeping its "disheveled dryad loveliness."[15] The transformation of the character of Faramir into a kind of replica of his brother Boromir is a huge mistake, but it seems to me to be in keeping with a general tendency to play down the nature of the gardener or steward role. Faramir is a wiser man than Boromir, "wise enough to know that there are some perils from which a man must flee."[16] He also is a gardener at heart. In the scene where (quite counter to the presentation in the film) he rejects the temptation of the Ring, he marvels at the hobbits and their Ring-bearing task and says:

"You are a new people and a new world to me. Are all your kin of like sort? Your land must be a realm of peace and content, and there must gardeners be in high honour."

"Not all is well there," said Frodo, "but certainly gardeners are honoured."[17]

And it is significant that Faramir's future is to marry Eowyn—the king's daughter of the Rohirrim who had proved herself as a warrior—and to become with her the chief tender of the restored garden of Ithilien. Listen to the conversation between them, which contrasts very clearly the two kinds of stories:

> I will be a shieldmaiden no longer, nor vie with the great Riders, nor take joy only in the songs of slaying. I will be a healer, and love all things that grow and are not barren. And again she looked at Faramir. "No longer do I desire to be a queen," she said.
>
> Then Faramir laughed merrily. "That is well," he said, "for I am not a king. Yet I will wed with the White Lady of Rohan, if it be her will. And if she will, then let us cross the River and in happier days let us dwell in fair Ithilien and there make a garden. All things will grow with joy there, if the White Lady comes."[18]

But the chief gardener—and, as others have argued, the true hero of the story—is Samwise Gamgee. It is Sam, after all, who returns to the homeland and stays put, who becomes four times mayor of the Shire, and who completes and passes on the story itself. We first meet Sam as a gardener, and a gardener he remains. Galadriel's gift to him in Lothlorien is a box containing fertile dust and a mallorn seed (recall Le Guin's argument that things to carry seed in are a more important image for story than swords).

> "For you little gardener and lover of trees," she said to Sam, "I have only a small gift." She put into his hand a little box of plain grey wood, unadorned save for a single silver rune upon the lid. "Here is set G for Galadriel," she said; "but also it may stand for garden in your tongue. ... It will not keep you on your road, nor defend you against any peril; but if you keep it and see your home again at last, then perhaps it may reward you. Though you should find all barren and laid waste, there will be few gardens in Middle-earth that will bloom like your garden, if you sprinkle this earth there. Then you may remember Galadriel, and catch a glimpse far off of Lórien, that you have seen only in our winter. For our Spring and our Summer are gone by, and they will never be seen on earth again save in memory."[19]

Of course Sam returns to a deeply wounded Shire: gardens neglected, land eroded, trees cut down. And he uses the contents of his box to restore the Shire to its garden state. And let it be said here, as a last complaint against the film's neglect of the unheroic gardener story, that the exclusion of the scouring of the Shire (its restoration as a place to be at home, to raise Elanor and all her siblings), is the movie's last serious compromise with the overall balance of Tolkien's great story.

So let me conclude. There are two kinds of story in *The Lord of the Rings:* the hero story and the gardener story. The first story—of the questing hero who leaves his home and battles enemies—is much easier to tell in film. The second, of tending, growth and daily love, is much harder, if not impossible, to convey in film. Both are worthy stories. Here Le Guin, it seems to me, is mistaken in suggesting that all hero stories are a kind of patriarchal perversion. There is a place and time for the warrior. But she is quite right in pointing out the great danger of failing to see that the seed-tending gardener, rather than the sword-wielding fighter, is a more basic picture of our humanity. Perhaps the greatest warrior of all in the story is Gandalf the wizard: but there is no doubt that he is a gardener, a steward first of all. He makes this point in the book in an important (and in the film, omitted) exchange with Denethor the steward, who is in danger of preferring his warrior-son Boromir's approach to his gardener-son Faramir's. Says Gandalf to him:

> [T]he rule of no realm is mine, neither of Gondor nor any other, great or small. But all worthy things that are in peril as the world now stands, those are my care. And for my part, I shall not wholly fail of my task, though Gondor should perish, if anything passes through this night that can still grow fair or bear fruit and flower again in days to come. For I also am a steward.[20]

This combination of power and service is very hard for us to understand today, and those critics who are uneasy with the film's tone of holy war are perhaps justified. But the accusation that *The Lord of the Rings* films elevate violence and destructive heroism cannot be leveled against the book. The whole shape of the story undercuts the accusation: the heroism of Gandalf, Aragorn, Boromir, the riders of Rohan and the rest are all, when it comes down to it, a diversion for the real world-changing action of the story, which is not about the exercise of power but the surrender of it. And it is at this point that Tolkien's profound grasp of the heart of the Christian story shows through most strongly. As he said many years ago in the lecture that is the occasion for this paper:

> The Gospels contain a fairy story, or a story of a larger kind which embraces all the essence of fairy stories . . . there is no tale ever told that men would rather find was true, and none which so many skeptical men have accepted as true on its own merits—this story is supreme and it is true. Art as been verified. God is the Lord of angels, and of men—and of elves. Legend and history have met and fused.[21]

It is a sad fact of history—and of our own time in particular—that the Christian story has been seen as an elevation of the warrior hero. There is a kind of heroism in that story, but it too is fundamentally about the giving up of power. "Lord" is a familiar term in Christian piety, but it is a dangerous one, and Christians would do well to remember that the "Lord" in *The Lord of the Rings* is Sauron the tyrant. The whole Christian story undercuts this concept of lordship: it too is about the giving up of power. Thus it is ironic today that an avowed enemy of Christianity like Philip Pullman in his "Dark Materials" trilogy calls the Christian God "the authority" and has its two child heroes destroy God as the Fellowship of the Ring destroys Sauron. Another great contemporary movie, Mel Gibson's *Passion of the Christ*, makes brutally plain that God's authority is rooted in suffering, not in the wielding of swords.

For the Christian story too is about the centrality of surrendering power—indeed, about gardening. Not only does the story begin in a garden but at its climax, the hero returning from his underground journey is rightly mistaken—as so many medieval portrayals show him—as a gardener. The unheroic gardener is the hero of Tolkien's story—and of the even greater Christian story that informs it. Perhaps necessarily, the medium of film fails when it tries to tell such a story.

Chapter 7

TOLKIEN'S AUGUSTINIAN UNDERSTANDING OF GOOD AND EVIL: WHY *THE LORD OF THE RINGS* IS NOT MANICHEAN

Ralph Wood

Enough books and essays have been written on *The Lord of the Rings* as a battle between good and evil to exhaust any need for further study along those lines. Yet, perhaps because of those many studies, a basic misunderstanding still persists—namely, that there is a strain of Manichean dualism at work in Tolkien, that he gives evil a power virtually equal to that of the good, and thus that his epic fantasy is so gloomy in both its final tone and ultimate implication that Christians are wrong to read it as a fictional parable or foreshadowing of the gospel.[1] It is certainly true that there is no real eucatastrophe in Tolkien's great work—no catastrophic ending in which, though much is destroyed, good totally triumphs. There is no event in Tolkien's work comparable to Christ's dyscatastrophic death issuing in his eucatastrophic resurrection.

Sauron the Sorcerer, the malign fashioner of the one Ruling Ring, is indeed defeated, and Middle-earth is wondrously spared his continuing depredations. Yet we are told that Sauron will assume some new and more sinister form in the future. The appendices reveal, in fact, that the Fourth Age, the age of men, proved to be hardly a better time than the Third Age of wizards and elves. The novel's penultimate episode is also quite muted in its cheer, as Gandalf and Frodo depart for the

Grey Havens in sheer exhaustion from their struggle, far too wounded to enjoy the fruits of their victory. It is a scene that only the flint-hearted can read without tears, and the sadness is hardly offset by Sam's welcome back to Hobbiton. No wonder that C. S. Lewis spoke of the enormous darkness of Tolkien's work. John Garth's recent study of Tolkien's devastating losses from the First War also underscores the fundamental tone of sadness pervading the whole of Tolkien's work.[2]

Yet such honest admissions are not cause to conclude, with Tom Shippey, that Tolkien's work is at once Augustinian and Manichean. The burden of this essay is to demonstrate instead that Tolkien's epic fantasy provides a powerful, convincing, and thoroughly Augustinian understanding of evil. To make this argument, I will first lay out Shippey's case for Tolkien's partial Manichaeism while setting it alongside Augustine's understanding of evil as *privatio boni*. Then I will seek to demonstrate that the workings of evil in Tolkien's epic fantasy have an altogether negative and derivative character, never assuming anything akin to equality with the good. The third section of the essay will attempt to show that, just as Tolkien's understanding of evil is thoroughly Augustinian, so is his vision for realizing the good equally congruous with the teachings of the Bishop of Hippo.

DUALISTIC AND MONOTHEISTIC CONCEPTIONS OF EVIL

Tom Shippey rightly discerns Tolkien's debt to St. Augustine's revolutionary insight (repeated by Boethius) that evil is *privatio boni*, the privation or absence of true being, the perversion or deformation of the good. Augustine deliberately guards against the deadly error of attributing divinity to evil, as if it were something inherent in God's good creation, or else as if it were some primordial force set over against and equal to God. Good and evil have no equivalence; rather, goodness and being share ontological status. It follows that no completely evil thing can have true life. Neither Morgoth nor Sauron was evil in the beginning. The things that they have spawned do not have true life; they are dreadful twistings and distortions of the good creation. Trolls are parodies of ents, the uruk-hai are mockeries of men, and the orcs are apes of elves. Yet even in its wretched malformation of the good, evil cannot escape acknowledging what it denies. As Shippey points out, the orcs themselves have an elementary conception of fairness, though of course "they are comically unable to apply it to themselves."[3]

Having got these complex matters exactly right, Shippey wrongly charges that Augustine (and Tolkien with him) renders evil potentially innocuous if not unreal by casting it in largely negative terms—as turning away from the larger to the lesser good, as worshipping the creation rather than the creator, and thus as making evil perhaps "more harmful to the malefactor than to the victim."[4] Shippey asks if evil is wholly negative and privative—often becoming the unintended means for realizing the intended good, as it often does in Tolkien—why resist it? Why not simply wait and let the forces of evil wear themselves out, eventually to vanish back into nothing, since so long as they are alive they will inevitably serve the good? The answer to this "extremely dangerous" teaching, as Shippey calls it, lies in Tolkien's alleged Manichaeism.

According to Shippey, Tolkien espouses not only a negative and Augustinian reading of the world's malificence, but also a positive and Manichean doctrine of evil. It can be discerned, Shippey insists, in Tolkien's granting of absolute and autonomous power to the Ring. In so doing, Tolkien creates a conflict "between the powers of Good and Evil, equal and opposite." Not only is there "no real difference" between these "supposedly opposing powers," Shippey argues; it is also "a matter of chance which side one happens to choose."[5]

Against Shippey's mistaken argument, I maintain that Tolkien is a radical anti-dualist whose Augustinian understanding of evil reveals it to be far more terrifying and dangerous than anything Manichaeism can imagine. Precisely because it has no proper basis, no true and logical existence, no explicable source, evil is horribly irrational—hence the Christian refusal to accord evil proper existence and even, in the strict sense, to "believe" in it. While every Christian gladly declares *Credo in Deus*, no orthodox creed has ever affirmed *Credo in diabolus*. We do not "believe" in the devil as if the demonic had free and self-sustaining existence. Nowhere in scripture, Karl Barth reminds us, do we find the words "Let there be darkness" but only "Let there be light." The God of light exists, moreover, without any darkness or "shadow of turning" (Jas 1:17). The fatal error of all Manichean and dialectical explanations of evil is that they make evil necessary to good, so that, without darkness and evil, goodness and light could not exist—the two "realities" serving as reciprocal and necessary halves of a greater whole.[6]

G. R. Evans suggests that Augustine was drawn to the Manichees, spending nine years as one of their adepts, precisely because they offered him scientific and philosophic respectability through a thoroughly rational account of the cosmos, especially of evil. By granting ontological status to wickedness alongside goodness, the Manichees solved the so-called problem of evil. Since God and his universe are entirely good—so runs the ancient question—whence evil? Evil can be identified with materiality, the Manichees answered, particularly with the body and all other things trapped in matter. Thus does evil have a standing virtually equal to that of the good, and thus does it make its perpetual war on the spiritual and immaterial world that supposedly constitutes the good.

To the young Augustine, the Manichean *Psalm-Book*—with its summons to cultivate a life of illumination by freeing one's soul from bodily desire—seemed very much akin to the Christianity he had learned from his mother. As a youth aflame with bodily passion, Augustine was drawn to the spiritual discipline of the Manichees; indeed, he practiced it so well that he was counted among their spiritual elite. Once he had combined a rigorous moral discipline with a highly intellectual account of the universe, Augustine had found exactly what he wanted: an exceedingly elevated opinion of his own intelligence as well as a convenient opacity to the new and subtler evil that was consuming him: pride. Thus was the young Augustine inclined to believe, writes Evans, that "there are two Natures, that of Light and that of Darkness. . . . Evil cannot alter the good, but it can crowd it on every side and impede its movement, for the good is not naturally warlike and it does not seek to meet evil with active opposition unless it recognises its danger."[7]

Gradually Augustine came to discern that the darkness of bodily passion does not confine the light; rather, it was the tangled strands of his own self-will that served to darken understanding. He was delivered from thralldom to the Manichees, therefore, only when he came to recognize that evil has no proper place in God's universe, that the root of evil lies in the corrupted will, that evil can be understood only as divine revelation discloses its meaning, and thus that "the very attempt to search for the cause of evil in the [intellectual] way he did was itself an evil thing."[8] "In my ignorance," Augustine admits, "I was disturbed by these questions [about the origin of evil], and while travelling away from the truth I thought I was going toward it. I did not know that evil has no existence except as a privation of good, down to that level which is altogether without being."[9]

Because evil is nowhere and no-thing, it defies rational explanation—at least in its origins. It has the quality of a *surd*, an irrational number, something having no justifiable cause, an existence that is essentially trivial and yet remains utterly destructive. Insofar as evil can be explained at all, it constitutes a mistaking of the creation for the creator. As St. Paul teaches in the first chapter of Romans, evil seeks to inveigle creatures into thus worshiping good things rather than honoring them as the good gift of their Maker. Though evil takes the form of twisted and distorted good—as in the original Edenic sin of a perverted desire for knowledge—there is never any true and compelling reason for the perversion. The aboriginal couple was given quite sufficient knowledge in the divine command to care for the garden and to eat the fruit of all the trees except the forbidden one. They had no need for omniscient, God-like knowledge. To do good was to obey God; to do evil was to deny his directive. Just as the serpent enters the garden without cause or explanation, so do Adam and Eve sin absurdly, wantonly, needlessly—abandoning all reason. It is dangerous, therefore, to explain evil in intellectual rather than volitional terms, for such alleged rationality leads to the delusion that, once evil is so understood, it can also be managed and controlled. On the contrary, as Augustine discovered, such intellectual attempts to comprehend the meaning of evil end by producing new evils of their own. As Evans declares: *"Deprivatio* is one thing—a mere absence; but *depravatio* is something altogether more fearsome in its positive potential for doing damage."[10]

THE COERCIVE POWERS OF THE RULING RING

Tolkien gives convincing fictional embodiment to these Augustinian claims. Morgoth had no cause for his rebellion against Ilúvatar, as if he had somehow been maltreated. It was from his own reasonless resentment that Morgoth sought to create a world of his own, and thus to introduce a terrible cacophony into the great symphonic Song of Creation that Eru was conducting into being. As Samuel Taylor Coleridge famously said of the evil that consumes Iago, Melkor is consumed by a "motiveless malignity." Yet Ilúvatar refuses to expel him from the heavenly court that is populated by the other fourteen valar. To cast him out of the divine realm would be to accord the evil Melkor even greater significance than he truly possesses. Melkor is allowed, instead, to enter Ilúvatar's newly created world called Eä along with the other valar. Foreshadowing the preeminence of mercy over justice that characterizes the whole of Tolkien's work, Ilúvatar refuses to answer Melkor's rebellion with rightful wrath. Instead, the mutinous vala is given the freedom to repent and thus once again to play his proper role in the magnificent symphonic work of the cosmos. Only when Melkor persists in his disobedience, becoming the wholly evil Morgoth, is he cast into the Void.

Unable to persuade others by means of either example or argument, the forces of evil must resort to deception and guile. And being devoid of the power to create, they must destroy. As Augustine taught, evil must corrupt good things by twisting and perverting them, giving them worth that is idolatrously absolute rather than humbly relative. Once evil is unleashed and sin becomes not deprivation but depravity, then death becomes Ilúvatar's merciful gift to humankind rather than a curse. Just as God drives our Edenic first parents out of the garden—lest they eat from the tree of eternal life and make their fallenness unending—so are Tolkien's human creatures gifted with merciful death. Thus does the Ring transform the unparalleled gift of life into the idol of deathlessness, so that its possessor will have ever greater quantitative but not qualitative existence. Bilbo declares, for example, that while the Ring has lengthened his years, it has not served to strengthen and enhance them; on the contrary, he feels weary and worn, "thin and stretched, like too little butter over too much bread."[11] There seems to be little doubt that, in the Sauronic temptation to live longer but not better, Tolkien is offering his own critical commentary on our death-fearing, life-worshipping culture.

The Ring's second negative but thoroughly pernicious power is to make its wearer invisible, thus overcoming the limits of bodily existence, especially the slowness and discipline and labor required in achieving all good things. Such invisible swiftness in accomplishment, though a boon for angels and other disembodied creatures, is a bane for mortals. It has made Gollum an idolater of food, perhaps the best of all gifts in the good creation. Utterly obsessed with eating, he dwells alone in the darkness of watery caves, catching endless fish and consuming them immediately in the raw—thus denying the fundament of civilization itself: the cooked and mutually shared meal. In constantly and greedily muttering to himself, moreover, Gollum has become a parody of authentic community, unable to enter relation with any other human or hobbitic creature.

For Tolkien, the Ring's power to confer invisibility is an evil kind of magic that finds its equivalent in modern culture, especially in the worship of the speed that technics enable. For Tolkien, all good and lasting things are created slowly and communally, with considerable time lapsing between their conception and their completion. The Company's initial journey to Rivendell is long and arduous, and the attempt to cross directly over Mount Caradhras proves disastrous. On all six occasions when Frodo actually puts on the Ring and thus achieves invisibility, he meets a far worse fate than if he had refused to do so. Whether in the making of meals or books, in marriages or friendships, in mastering skills or developing convictions, all worthy things flourish and endure to the extent that they take shape gradually, without recourse to shortcuts, especially to the time-crunching means made available by our late-modern kind of invisibility—namely, technological instantaneity.

Thus far Shippey would perhaps find little cause for dissent, since he admits that one aspect of Tolkien's account of evil is a Boethian and Augustinian account of evil as perverted good. Yet the Ring has a third power, the one that has led Shippey and others to allege it to be Manichean: it can overwhelm the creature's freedom. When Melkor and Sauron and their minions cannot succeed by perverting and dissembling, they resort to sheer compulsion—not only to the outward and visible forces of the orc-and-warg hosts and to the Uruk-hai armies, but also to the inward and invisible coercions of the will. Shippey is thus correct to interpret the Ring as overpowering Frodo's will at the Cracks of Mount Doom. It is not the weak and emaciated hobbit who speaks in a loud and stentorian voice when he reaches the moment of final decision to cast the Ring back into the volcanic fires whence it was originally forged; it is another voice altogether: "I have come. . . . But I do not choose now to do what I came to do. I will not do this deed. The Ring is mine."[12] Frodo's freedom is utterly flattened. He is completely overwhelmed by a force greater even than Sauron, as the ventriloquizing Ring declares its own imperious will through the mouth of the helpless hobbit.

This would seem to be evidence of the rankest sort of Manichaeism. Frodo's final act of refusal appears to be prompted not by his own perversions and distortions of the good but by the autonomous and overwhelming power of the Ring. What Shippey and like-minded critics fail to discern, however, is that temptation and compulsion are not opposite but complementary operations of evil. The slightest peccadillo undertaken out of mere curiosity—perhaps in the first snort of cocaine—often creates a further desire for the mild pleasure that it initially afforded. This second acquiescence to the allurements of ecstasy further closes the window of freedom, alas, as mere velleity gradually becomes drastic necessity. Soon the will that had acted initially without compulsion is itself compelled, addicted, trapped.[13] Even as noble a character as Bilbo suffers such compulsion even from his few uses of the Ring. It comes to have an imprisoning grip on his volition, so that he finds it ever so difficult to hand the Ring over to Gandalf, as he threatens violence against his altogether benign wizard-friend.

Yet Frodo's case is not parallel to Bilbo's. He has used the Ring with ever less frequency as the Quest progresses, its addictive powers seeming not to have debilitated his resistance. Yet the nearer he and Sam approach Sammath Naur—the "chambers of fire" high in the core of Mt. Orodruin where Sauron forged the One Ring in the Cracks of Doom—the greater the burden and power of the Ruling Ring. It has not only rendered Frodo physically emaciated; it has also drained his spirit, leaving him with an overwhelming sense of hopelessness. The dread fear that he will not succeed in his mission, especially as the obstacles to his errand increase in fury and horror, infects Frodo with a deep pessimism. The Ring absorbs every moment of consciousness, whether he is awake or asleep: "I begin to see it in my mind all the time, like a great wheel of fire. . . . I am naked in the dark, Sam, and there is no veil between me and the wheel of fire. I begin to see it even with my waking eyes, and all else fades."[14]

Such a seemingly Manichean scene raises a hard question: whence does such soul-deadening, will-quashing power derive? Shippey sees the Ring's evil as having transcendent and autonomous status, as if it existed in quasi-dualistic relation to the good. Tolkien offers a clear counter-answer: such bullying coercions originate from the rebellious wills of such once-good creatures as Melkor and Sauron, as Saruman and Sméagol. Individual acts of revolt and rebellion gradually acquire social and political character, just as in scripture the seemingly small sin of eating the forbidden fruit acquires such terrible magnitude that Yahweh is finally compelled to drown virtually the whole creation, lest personal sin become systemic and pandemic evil. The destruction of the Tower of Babel is yet another example of personal rebellion taking on culture-wide proportions, as Yahweh again puts a halt to man's sinful attempt to create a single, dominant culture and language.[15]

So it is in Tolkien. The sun-blighting and will-enslaving atmosphere of Mordor has a distinctively modern quality. Sauron's is truly an evil empire. Tolkien repeatedly described his own age as the most oppressive in human history. The various totalitarianisms of the previous century tyrannized the human spirit with unprecedented coercive power. In addition to the multiplied millions who were slaughtered by their own governments, many more were made to live in constant fear of offending their repressive overlords and thus of bringing terror upon themselves. The allegedly "free" nations of the democratic West have their own compulsions, of course. As materialistic cultures of comfort and convenience, of abortion and euthanasia, of mind-altering drugs and hyper-eroticized entertainment, they enslave their own inhabitants, albeit largely unawares.[16] Tolkien seems clearly to suggest that the human spirit—even when figured at its best in Frodo at the Cracks of Doom—should never be subjected to such hideous pressures.

It should be evident that Shippey's most serious mistake is to identify outward and hostile forces with Manichaeism, while limiting the Boethian-Augustinian understanding of evil to inward and alluring temptation.[17] He seems not to recognize that social evils no less than personal sins are perversions of the good, and thus that those too must be accounted for in Augustinian terms. Such evils are not the work of Manichean powers of material malificence invading the so-called passive spiritual forces of good; they are the demonic outworking of collective human disobedience. This is precisely the point of the doctrine of original sin as Augustine, following Paul, helped to formulate it: we are born into a social matrix of evil that precedes and induces our own personal commission of sin, even though we also remain individually responsible for assenting to the living of sinful lives.

Tolkien makes the social character of evil evident from the beginning. Idyllic though the Shire surely seems, it is far from a sinless place. Frodo's own orphaning, we learn, may have been the result of a double murder. Hobbiton itself, though an ever-so-pleasant place, is also rife with gossip and suspicion. Thus does the Shire eventually fall prey to the temptations of Saruman, Wormtongue, and the other Sauronic deceivers. The agrarian countryside is turned into an industrial wasteland, the pubs are closed in a grim denial of communal festivity, and a massive repressive bureaucracy is installed, so that spying neighbor is set against spying neighbor. Upon seeing the sorry condition of the Shire following their yearlong absence, Frodo and Sam have perhaps the darkest exchange in the entire epic: "'This is worse than Mordor,'" said Sam. "Much worse in a way. It comes home to you, as they say; because it is home, and you remember it before it was all ruined." "Yes, this is Mordor," said Frodo. "Just one of its works."[18]

THE FELLOWSHIP OF THE FREE AS THE ANSWER TO BULLYING EVIL

Because evil is social and communal, the remedy against it is also social and communal. Frodo and Sam and the other members of the Fellowship do not seek mere personal deliverance in their Quest to destroy the Ruling Ring: they undertake the salvation of the Shire itself, the community without which there can be no good of any kind. Augustine writes his *magnum opus* in defense of the church as precisely such a community: the *civitas* that alone can provide a redeeming alternative to the oppressions of the Roman *imperium*. Though Augustine would never equate the church militant with the *civitas dei*, neither would he treat it as an institution that remains peripheral, much less inessential, for salvation. To be a Christian, he taught, is to belong to the body of Christ. There is no such thing as solitary or private salvation; on the contrary, Augustine would have regarded such late-modern individualism as the essence of heresy.

In fact, there is no salvation outside the church, as St. Cyprian had declared in the third century: *extra ecclesiam nulla salus*. Following Paul, Augustine insisted that Christians constitute the body of Christ because they have been "baptized into" it (1 Cor 12:13), and that the risen Lord is a complete and living person whose body is the church. What keeps this claim from being unpardonably hubristic is the church's confession, as Robert Jenson explains, that Christians "jointly intend Christ not as ourselves, but as the sacramental objects [that is, baptism and eucharist] in our midst. Using a famous distinction of modern sociology, the church as a *community* is the body of Christ in that the church as an association is confronted within herself by the body of Christ—the same body of Christ that she as community is."[19]

In creating an imaginative pre-Christian realm such as Middle-earth—where there is not yet a chosen people nor an incarnate Messiah—Tolkien cannot place a sacramental community in its midst, but he can and does provide a large analogy to it in the Fellowship of the Nine Walkers. The Trinitarian quality of their number seems unmistakable, even if it also signifies their opposition to the Nine Riders, the cloned clutch of mortal men who, by using the rings that Sauron made for them, have become terrifying wraiths enslaved to the Dark Lord.

In yet another mark of his anti-Manichaeism, Tolkien demonstrates the impossibility of a true community of evil, a real fellowship of the wicked. The orcs are always quarreling and competing selfishly against each other, often enabling the good to happen inadvertently. Sauron is served by slaves who abjectly submit to their master. Never can it be said of the Necromancer and his thralls what Jesus says of his own disciples: "I do not call you servants any longer, because the servant does not know what the master is doing; but I have called you friends, because I have made known to you everything that I have heard from my Father" (John 15:15). There are collectivities of evil, of course, and they are formed by those who have criminal things in common. Yet there is no true fellowship of the vicious, however rigidly loyal its members may be. Whether in the Taliban or al-Qaida, in the Mafia or street gangs, in Sauron or Saruman, there is no company of the free but only of the fearful.

Shippey finds the apparent binary opposition between the Nine Riders and the Nine Walkers to be implicitly Manichean, declaring that "both good and evil function as external powers and as inner impulses from the psyche." He is troubled, moreover, that "while the balances are maintained, we are on the whole more conscious of evil as an objective power and of good as a subjective impulse. Mordor and 'the Shadow' are nearer and more visible than the Valar" and the other providential powers at work in Middle-earth.[20] Surely the answer to Shippey's objection is that the seeming weakness exhibited by the servants of the good serves to *underscore* the anti-Manichean quality of Tolkien's work. If Tolkien's imagination were even residually Manichean, the scene at Sammath Naur would have become the occasion for an all-out battle between the matching forces of good and evil.

Yet it is precisely such swaggering power that Tolkien, as a Christian, denies to Ilúvatar. Eru (as he is also called) is not a bellicose divinity of brute and visible might; he is precisely the opposite. He refuses autocratically to impose his will. Working often invisibly through his agents called the valar and maiar, Eru refuses ruthlessly to quash evil—just as he refused to cast the rebel Melkor out of the heavenly realm but rather allowed him to enter Eä despite his ruination of the Music of the Ainur. Ilúvatar and his free servants will not perform mirror-image replications of Morgoth's coercive acts. They are determined, instead, to overcome evil with good—with the free cooperative agency of their human and elvish, their dwarfish and hobbitic allies—even if their final victory requires the totality of time.

The Nine Walkers are chosen, rather like Jesus' own disciples, not because they are stalwart heroes but because they possess gifts that, when rightly ordered and directed to the good, serve well in a battle that is more about losing than winning—since their mission is to surrender rather than to employ the Ring of coercive power. These nine creatures are a remarkable community of the unlike. Just as Jesus' original followers are meant to represent the twelve tribes of Israel, so do the Nine Walkers represent all the free peoples of Middle-earth: a wizard, an elf, a dwarf, two men, and four hobbits. They are united not by race or ethnicity or class, but solely by their common devotion to each other and their Quest. Far from being a mere "subjective impulse," as Shippey alleges, the company of the good is animated by the three theological virtues. Their mission is finally accomplished by way of their faithful and trusting community, their hopeful conviction that the Quest will succeed even if they themselves fail, and their loving, forgiving solidarity—even with their enemies.

Elrond chooses Gandalf for his wisdom, Aragorn because of his ancestral link to the Ring, Boromir for his valor, Legolas for his elvish mastery of the woods, Gimli for his dwarvish knowledge of mountains and mines, Frodo because he is "the best hobbit of the Shire," and Sam because he is Frodo's closest companion. Merry and Pippin are added simply because they refuse to be parted with Frodo. When Elrond objects that these two youngsters cannot imagine the terrors that surely lie ahead, Gandalf reminds him that they possess a more important quality: "It is true that if these hobbits understood the danger, they would not dare to go. But they would still wish to go, or wish that they dared, and be shamed and unhappy. I think, Elrond, that in this matter it would be well to trust rather to their friendship than to great wisdom."[21]

The faith that produces trusting friendship—faith in each other no less than their common mission—is one of the prime means by which communal good is realized in *The Lord of the Rings.* Aristotle called friendship the excellence that is "most indispensable for life." It is literally the company's *sine qua non:* without it they would be literally nothing. It unites them in the beginning, sustains them throughout their long ordeal, and enables the final success of the Quest at the end. As in scripture, so in Tolkien is the Fellowship a frail and sinful community. Its unity is broken not by orcs or trolls but by one of its own members, Boromir, who in a Peter-like betrayal tries to achieve quick victory over Sauron by seizing and using the Ring to defeat him. His attempt at an individualist kind of heroism is exactly the heroism that Tolkien repudiates. The company always works in concert, never by way of solitary effort. Even after Boromir's betrayal, the Fellowship functions as small sub-communities of two or three members.

Nowhere is this figured more vividly than in Merry's early declaration of solidarity with Frodo: "You can trust us to stick with you through thick and thin—to the bitter end. And you can trust us to keep any secret of yours—closer than you keep it yourself. But you cannot trust us to let you face trouble alone, and go off without a word. We are your friends, Frodo."[22] With those four plain monosyllables, had Sauron heard and fathomed them, his mighty fortress at Barad-dûr would have been shaken to its foundations. For none other than this trusting community of friends will enable the final overthrow of the seemingly impregnable stronghold of the master Force-Wielder. For the Dark Lord can never enter friendship; he can prompt only fear in those who are enslaved to him. If he possessed positive and thus Manichean power, he could form at least a rudimentary community.

Not perfect love alone but true hope, Tolkien shows, can also cast out fear. Samwise Gamgee, the least reflective of the hobbits, comes to discern the nature of this hope most clearly. In the Tower of Cirith Ungol, as he and Frodo have begun to doubt whether their Quest will ever succeed—and thus to fear that they will die and be utterly forgotten—Sam seeks to distinguish between tales that really matter and those that do not, and thus to locate the one hope-giving story. He admits that, had they known how hard would be the road that lay ahead of them, they would never have come at all. Yet such is the way of stories, he adds, that rivet the mind and of songs that are sung for the ages. They are not about fellows who set out on adventures of their own choosing, Sam confesses, but about folks who found themselves traveling a path that they would have never have elected to follow. And even though such pilgrims were chosen for the Quest, they could have turned back. If so, no one would have ever sung their story, since those who defect from their calling are not celebrated. What counts, Sam wisely warns, is not that these heroes defeated their enemies and returned home safely to relish their triumph, but that they soldiered ahead and slogged forward to whatever end awaited them, whether good or ill.

THE ANTI-MANICHEAN PITY OF BILBO AND FRODO

If it is not a happy ending that matters, then what does? After all, each particular human story—and, by extension, the stories of all fellowships and companies—will finally finish and permanently disappear. As we have noticed from the appendices, the Fourth Age did not issue in any ongoing triumph of the good. Does this mean that all stories are equal— perhaps equally futile and vain? Not at all, says Sam. What matters is whether our own small stories contribute to an infinitely larger story and thus whether we rightly enact our own small roles within the grand saga. If we do, Sam adds, then when our own little story is done, some other actor will take the tale forward to either a better or worse moment in the ongoing drama. In this infinitely larger story that encompasses all the smaller stories, nothing is lost. As Tolkien declares in *The Silmarillion* that "beauty not before conceived [shall] be brought into Eä, and *evil yet be good to have been*."[23]

Sam is required to test this paradoxical and radical hope when he and Frodo are nearing Mordor and thus the end of their long and wearisome journey. All their efforts seem finally to have failed. Even if somehow they succeed in destroying the Ring, there is no likelihood that they will survive or that anyone will ever hear of their valiant deed. They seem doomed to oblivion. Yet amidst such apparent hopelessness, Sam beholds a single star shimmering above the dark clouds of Mordor: "The beauty of it smote his heart, as he looked up out of the forsaken land, and hope returned to him. For like a shaft, clear and cold, the thought pierced him that in the end the Shadow was only a small and passing thing: there was light and high beauty for ever beyond its reach."[24]

Shippey is right to insist that in *The Lord of the Rings* the powers of evil are made to appear far more palpable and real than do the powers of good. The vast darkened sky of Mordor, illumined by only a single star, would seem to signal not even a Manichean balance of forces but the triumph of evil once and for all. Such, however, is the danger of appearances in a world whose powers are depicted in an Augustinian manner. Going far beyond the obvious, Sam discerns the deep truth that star and shadow are not locked in a dualistic combat of evils. Light is both the primal and the final reality, not the darkness that seeks to confine and quench it. The single flickering star, Sam sees, both penetrates and identifies the gargantuan gloom. So it is with all of the other apparent binaries: there is not balance but paradoxical asymmetry between them. Hope defines despair, friendship defines enmity, salvation defines damnation.

Tolkien makes this Augustinian imbalance of opposites especially manifest in the privileging of love—understood as pity and mercy and forgiveness—as the central virtue of *The Lord of the Rings*. The summons to pity is voiced most clearly by Gandalf after Frodo expresses his outrage that Bilbo had the chance to kill the wicked Gollum but did not. Frodo has cause for his fury. Gollum was indeed seeking to slay Bilbo, and had Bilbo not put on the Ring to escape him, there is little doubt that Gollum would have murdered Frodo's kinsman. Why, asks Frodo, should Bilbo not have given Gollum the justice he so fully deserved? Gandalf answers with a speech that lies at the moral and religious center of the entire epic:

> [Frodo:] "What a pity that Bilbo did not stab that vile creature when he had a chance!"
>
> [Gandalf:] "Pity? It was Pity that stayed his hand. Pity, and Mercy: not to strike without need. And he has been well rewarded, Frodo. Be sure that [Bilbo] took so little hurt from the evil, and escaped in the end, because he began his ownership of the Ring so. With Pity."
>
> "I am sorry," said Frodo. "But I am frightened; and I do not feel any pity for Gollum."
>
> "You have not seen him," Gandalf broke in.
>
> "No, and I don't want to," said Frodo. . . . Now at any rate he is as bad as an Orc, and just an enemy. He deserves death."
>
> "Deserves it! I daresay he does. Many that live deserve death. And some that die deserve life. Can you give it to them? Then do not be too eager to deal out death in judgement. For even the very wise cannot see all ends. I have not much hope that Gollum can be cured before he dies, but there is a chance of it. And he is bound up with the fate of the Ring. My heart tells me that he has some part to play yet, for good or ill, before the end; and when that comes, the pity of Bilbo may rule the fate of many—yours not the least."[25]

"The pity of Bilbo may rule the fate of many" is the only declaration to be repeated in all three volumes of The Lord of the Rings. It is indeed the *leitmotif* of Tolkien's epic, its animating theme, its Augustinian epicenter as well as its circumference. Gandalf's prophecy is true in the literal sense, for the same vile Gollum whom Bilbo had spared long ago finally, albeit unintentionally, enables the Ring's destruction—when, in a dance of delirious joy at having bitten the Ring from Frodo's finger, he falls into the fiery fissure. The wizard's saying is also true in the spiritual sense. For in this speech Gandalf lays out a decidedly non-Manichean notion of mercy. As a creature far more sinning than sinned against, Gollum deserves his misery. He has committed Cain's sin in acquiring the Ring, having slain his cousin in jealous desire for it. Yet while the Ring extended Gollum's life by five centuries and enabled him endlessly to relish raw fish, it has also made him utterly wretched. Far from requiring a Manichean opposite to reveal its nature, evil remains its own worst torment, as Gandalf reminds Frodo in this crucial early scene: "You have not seen him."

There is still a deeper reason for Gandalf's insistence on pity. In response to Frodo's demand that Gollum be given justice, the wizard offers a profound reading of mercy as the one remedy to Gollum's desolate condition. If all died who deserved punishment, says Gandalf, surely none would live. Many perish, he adds, who are worthy of life, and yet who can restore them? Gandalf supplies the answer to his own rhetorical question: none. Be exceedingly chary, he warns, about judging others by any standard other than the one that has somehow spared Frodo himself. Though Gandalf speaks of sentencing Gollum and others to literal death, there are many kinds of death—scorn, contempt, neglect, dismissal—that such judgment could also render. Frodo is in danger, Gandalf sees, of committing the subtlest and deadliest of all sins: self-righteousness. "Do not Judge, so that you may not be judged. For with the judgment you make you will be judged, and the measure you give will be the measure you get" (Matt 7:1).

If Frodo assesses Gollum by any other criterion than his own escape from well-deserved punishment—insisting that Gollum be given justice, when Frodo himself has been given grace—he is in dread danger of presumption. Neither hobbits nor humans, Tolkien suggests, can live by the bread of merit alone. Gollum is not to be executed, though he may well deserve death, precisely because he is a fellow sinner, a fallen creature of feeble frame, a comrade in the stuff of dust. Gandalf admits that there is not much hope for Gollum's return to the creaturely circle, but neither is there much hope for many others, perhaps not even for most. To deny them such mercy, Gandalf concludes, is to deny it also to oneself.

Gandalf's discourse on pity marks the huge distance between Tolkien's book and not only the Manichean world of the ancient East but also the heroic world of the ancient West. Among most pagan cultures—like their modern counterparts—pity is not a virtue. The Greeks, for example, extend pity only to the pathetic, the helpless, those who are able to do little or nothing for themselves. When Aristotle says that the function of tragic drama is to arouse fear and pity, he refers to the fate of a character such as Oedipus. We are to fear that his fate might somehow be ours, and we are to pity him for the ineluctable circumstances of his life. But pity is never to be given to the heinous and undeserving, for such mercy would deny them the justice that they surely merit. Mercy of this kind—the kind so central to Augustinian faith—would indeed be a vice.

According to the warrior ethic of antique Germanic and Scandinavian cultures, the offering of pardon to enemies is unthinkable: they must be utterly defeated. For Tolkien the Augustinian Christian, by contrast, love understood as mercy and pity is essential: "You have heard that it was said, 'You shall love your neighbor and hate your enemy.' But I say to you, Love your enemies and pray for those who persecute you. . . . For if you love those who love you, what reward do you have?" (Matt 5:43-44, 46). Here we see the crucial distinction between *philia* as the love of friends who share our deepest concerns, and *agape* as the love of those who are not only radically "other" to us, but who deserve our wrath and who cannot reciprocate our pardon. We can make friends only with those whose convictions we share, but Christians are called to have pity for those whom we do not trust, even and especially our enemies. No wonder, then, that Sam ends his discourse on stories by suggesting that even the shadow-side of every human and hobbitic story finds its surprising place in the One story: "Why," says Sam, "even Gollum might be good in a tale."[26]

So it is that Tolkien's work remains not at all Manichean but thoroughly Augustinian. Because evil is no-thing, it can assume any form it wishes, and the more deceptive its means, the more successful its ends. The struggle against evil thus requires enormous faith and fortitude, supreme subtlety and hope, but above all the power of undeserved mercy. These salutary means of mortal resistance to demonic coercion are also Tolkien's own means for establishing the profoundest truth of his epic fantasy: the Lord of the Rings is not a coercive Manichean force such as Sauron but the Augustinian creator of all things good and of none evil: Ilúvatar, together with his humble servants and friends.

NOTES

Chapter 1

*   I am indebted to Kirstin Johnson for her enthusiastic encouragement in this writing up of the exhibition mounted in connection with the ITIA Symposium to celebrate the sixty-fifth anniversary of the delivery in St. Andrews of J. R. R. Tolkien's Andrew Lang Lecture on 8 March 1939.

1   J. R. R. Tolkien, *The Letters of J. R. R. Tolkien*, ed. Humphrey Carpenter (London: HarperCollins, 1999), 220 [165, undated, to Houghton Mifflin].

2   University of St. Andrews muniments, UYUY452/41/80. The use of this and subsequent extracts is by kind permission of the Keeper of Muniments of the University of St. Andrews.

3   University of St. Andrews muniments, UYUY452/40/87, 94, 96.

4   Copy out-letter from Andrew Bennett, Secretary to the University Court, to J. R. R. Tolkien, 8 October 1938 (University of St. Andrews muniments UYUY7Sec/1b/118). It is interesting to note that the stipend was reduced to £20 in 1951/52 due to an over-expenditure of proceeds from the original investment, as shown in Senatus Minute 1951/52, 94 (UYUY7Sec/2/file 404).

5   University of St. Andrews muniments, copy out-letter books, UYUY7 Sec/1b/118–19. The date of the lecture has been erroneously recorded by Tolkien as 1940 in J. R. R. Tolkien, "On Fairy-Stories," in *Essays Presented to*

Charles Williams, ed. C. S. Lewis (London: Oxford University Press, 1947); and 1938 in J. R. R. Tolkien, *Tree and Leaf: Including the Poem Mythopoeia, the Homecoming of Beorhtnoth Beorhthelm's Son* (London: HarperCollins, 2001).

6   *Concerning Andrew Lang, Being the Andrew Lang Lectures Delivered before the University of St. Andrews, 1927–1937*, ed. A. Blyth Webster and J. B. Salmond (Oxford: Clarendon, 1949), vii.

7   *Concerning Andrew Lang*, viii.

8   See "On Fairy-Stories," 38. The title was changed to "On Fairy-Stories" when the lecture appeared in print, cf. *The St. Andrews Citizen*, 11 March 1939: 4. "'Fairy-Stories' was the title chosen by Professor J. R. R. Tolkien . . . for the eleventh in the series of lectures under the Andrew Lang Foundation."

9   Humphrey Carpenter, *J. R. R. Tolkien: A Biography* (London: HarperCollins, 2002), 221. Farmer Giles was later revised and published in a fuller form, illustrated by Pauline Baynes.

10   Carpenter, *A Biography*, 253.

11   *Letters of J. R. R. Tolkien*, 310 [234, 22 November 1961, to Jane Neave].

12   Brian Rosebury, *J. R. R. Tolkien: A Critical Assessment* (Basingstoke: Macmillan, 1992), 81.

13   Randel Helms, *Tolkien's World* (Boston: Houghton Mifflin, 1974), 11.

14   William H. Green, *The Hobbit: A Journey into Maturity* (New York: Twayne Publishers, 1995), 20.

15   Green, *The Hobbit*, 21.

16   Michael White, *Tolkien: A Biography* (London: Abacus, 2002), 175.

17   Rosebury, 5.

18   Carpenter, *A Biography*, 255.

19   Gilbert Murray, *Andrew Lang the poet: being the Andrew Lang lecture delivered before the University of St. Andrews, 7 May 1947* (London: Oxford University Press, 1948); Hugh Pattison Macmillan, and Baron Macmillan, *Law and Custom: being the Andrew Lang lecture delivered before the University of St. Andrews, 5 April 1948* (Edinburgh: Nelson & Sons, 1949). See also, e.g., James Fergusson, *Shakespeare's Scotland: being the Andrew Lang lecture delivered before the University of St. Andrews, 14 November 1956* (Edinburgh: Thomas Nelson & Sons, 1957).

20   "Tolkien had a passion for perfection in written work of any kind, whether it be philology or stories. This grew from his emotional commitment to his work, which did not permit him to treat it in any manner other than the deeply serious. Nothing was allowed to reach the printed until it had been revised, reconsidered and polished." Carpenter, *A Biography*, 186.

21 In a letter to Sir Stanley Unwin dated 21 July 1946 (*Letters of J. R. R. Tolkien*, 118 [105]), Tolkien says he is "about to publish a much expanded version of an essay on Fairy stories, originally delivered as a lecture at St. Andrews, in a memorial volume to the late Charles Williams." The lecture was reworked again by Tolkien himself in retirement and published along with "Leaf by Niggle" in Tolkien, *Tree and Leaf*.

22 T. Malcolm Knox was professor of moral philosophy at St. Andrews, 1936–1952, acting principal of the university 1952–1953, and its principal 1953–1966. This letter was the subject of an article by Meic Pierce Owen, "Tolkien and St. Andrews," *University of St. Andrews Staff Newsletter* January 2004, 1–3. J. R. R. Tolkien, "Letter to Professor T. Malcom Knox," University of St. Andrews, ms37525/512.

23 Wayne G. Hammond and Douglas Anderson (assistant), *J. R. R. Tolkien: A Descriptive Bibliography* (Winchester: St. Paul's Bibliographies, 1993), 300–301.

24 UYLY accession record 199,189, classmark PN36.W5.

25 *St. Andrews Citizen*, 11 March 1939, 4.

26 Tolkien, *Essays Presented to Charles Williams*, 38.

27 *Letters of J. R. R. Tolkien*, 343 [254, 9 January 1964, Tolkien to Rev. Denis Tyndall].

28 St. Andrews University Calendar, 1966–1967, 712.

29 Developed by the library during the present century from existing stock, with additional purchases from time to time, the Lang Collection totals over 430 volumes of works by and edited by Andrew Lang (1844–1912), Scottish man of letters and student at St. Andrews from 1861 to 1863. The Collection is strong in his first editions, and was greatly augmented by a bequest of over 200 volumes from Roger Lancelyn Green in 1989. There is also a substantial holding of Lang manuscripts including over 1000 letters and over 50 literary and miscellaneous manuscripts and proofs.

30 See the definitive article, Roger Lancelyn Green, "Andrew Lang and the Fairy Tale," *Review of English Studies* 20 (1944).

31 Carpenter, *A Biography*, 39. First published as Andrew Lang, *Red Fairy Book* (London: Longmans, Green, 1890).

32 Tolkien, *Tree and Leaf*, 36, 39.

33 Carpenter, *A Biography*, 39.

34 Tolkien, *Tree and Leaf*, 41.

35 Simon Houfe, *The Dictionary of British Book Illustrators and Caricaturists 1800–1914* (Woodbridge: Baron Publishing, 1978), 306–7. See also Victor Watson, ed., *The Cambridge Guide to Children's Books in English* (Cambridge:

Cambridge University Press, 2001) 165: "H. J. Ford's 'pre-Raphaelite' illustrations, which still accompany most editions of the *Fairy Books*, add immeasurably to the sense of the enchanted world that one enters in the tales themselves."

36 It is interesting to note that in 1976, when Brian Alderson edited *Red Fairy Book* for publication by Kestrel Books, he chose to omit "The Story of Sigurd" from the collection, following the lead of Lang himself whose original introduction apologized for "turning back into fairy tale the splendid saga of Sigurd." Cf. Brian Alderson, ed., *Red Fairy Book, Collected by Andrew Lang* (Harmondsworth: Kestrel, 1976).

37 Wayne G. Hammond and Christina Scull, *J. R. R. Tolkien: Artist and Illustrator* (London: HarperCollins, 1995), 50, 53, 136–40.

38 A rather elusive booklet that forms the proceedings of the fourth Tolkien Society workshop held at the Friary, Beverley on 24 June 1989 and published by the Tolkien Society in Christina Scull, "Dragons from Andrews Lang's Retelling of Sigurd to Tolkien's Chrysophylax," *Leaves from the Tree: J. R. R. Tolkien's Shorter Fiction* (London: The Tolkien Society, 1991), 49–62.

39 Letter to W. H. Auden, 7 June 1955, in *Letters of J. R. R. Tolkien*, 214 [163].

40 Hammond and Scull, 53.

41 Hammond and Scull, 136, quoting from manuscript of the lecture in the Bodleian Library. See also *Letters of J. R. R. Tolkien*, 27 [19, 16 December 1937 to Stanley Unwin].

42 Christopher Tolkien, *Pictures by J. R. R. Tolkien* (London: HarperCollins, 1992), 17.

43 Hammond and Scull, 107.

44 J. S. Ryan, "Two Oxford Scholars' Perceptions of the Traditional Germanic Hall," in *Minas Tirith Evening-Star* 19, no. 1 (1990): 8–11.

45 Hammond and Scull, 109, 120, 122–23.

46 Michael White's 2001 biography of Tolkien does acknowledge that his vision of the dragon was heavily influenced by his childhood love of the *Red Fairy Book* by Andrew Lang, which contained a particularly dramatic dragon tale called "Sigurd and Fáfnir" (121). However, White makes no specific reference to the striking visual similarities between the 1890 depiction of Fáfnir and Tolkien's 1937 representation of Smaug. William H. Green sees Smaug as a synthesis of sources: Beowulf's dragon, the Old Norse Fáfnir, classic heraldic representation of a dragon, the flying dragon from Malory's *Le Morte d'Arthur*, but closest to Spenser's dragon in *The Faerie Queene*, book 1, canto 11.

47 The narrative similarity of the stories of Sigurd and Bilbo, of Fáfnir and Smaug was acknowledged by Tolkien in a letter to Naomi Mitchison dated 18 December 1949 (*Letters of J. R. R. Tolkien*, 134 [122]): "I find 'dragons' a fascinating product of imagination. But I don't think the *Beowulf* one is frightfully good. But the whole problem of the intrusion of the 'dragon' into northern imagination and its transformation there is one I do not know enough about. Fáfnir in the late Norse versions of the Sigurd-story is better, and Smaug and his conversation obviously is in debt there." However, as T. A. Shippey notes, "as often, Tolkien took the hints, but felt he could improve on them." *J. R. R. Tolkien: Author of the Century* (Boston: Houghton Mifflin, 2001), 37.

48 See *Letters of J. R. R. Tolkien*, 31 [25, undated, to the editor of the "Observer']. The full quotation is: "The dragon bears a name—a pseudonym—the past tense of the primitive Germanic verb *smugan*, to squeeze through a hole: a low philological jest."

49 David Day and Lidia Postma (illustrator), *The Hobbit Companion* (London: Pavillion Books, 2002), 68–69.

50 Carpenter, *A Biography*, 237–38.

Chapter 2

1 E. M. W. Tillyard and C. S. Lewis, *The Personal Heresy: A Controversy* (Oxford: Oxford University Press, 1965).

2 Tolkien, *Tree and Leaf*.

3 Colin Manlove, *Christian Fantasy: From 1200 to the Present* (Notre Dame, Ind.: University of Notre Dame Press, 1992).

4 Cf. J. R. R. Tolkien, *The Lost Road and Other Writings*, ed. Christopher Tolkien (London: HarperCollins, 1992), 45.

5 Owen Barfield, *Poetic Diction: A Study in Meaning*, 2nd ed. (London: Faber & Faber, 1962).

6 C. S. Lewis, *Rehabilitations and Other Essays* (London: Oxford University Press, 1939), 81–82.

7 Ed. note: On Tolkien's presentation of good and evil, see Ralph Wood's essay in this volume.

Chapter 3

1 *Letters of J. R. R. Tolkien*, 220 [165, undated, to Houghton Mifflin].

2 *Letters of J. R. R. Tolkien*, 310 [234, 22 November 1961, to Jane Neave].

3 Tolkien, *Tree and Leaf*, v.

4   "On Fairy-Stories" in *Tree and Leaf*, 54.

5   There are those who are more circumspect with the term: "The Mythopoeic Society," which began as a Tolkien society over forty years ago, has earned due recognition for their contribution to scholarship on the works of "The Inklings" and other like-minded writers, and for their encouragement of authors whose work the Society deems mythopoeic.

6   The *OED* defines *mythopoeic* as: "Myth-making; productive of myths; pertaining to the creation of myths." It is probably worth noting here that while Tolkien himself did work for Oxford University Press on the *Oxford English Dictionary* (primarily contributing to the "W" section), he was at times quite dissatisfied with the definitions found therein; he makes particular note of this in regard to the word *faery*. "On Fairy-Stories" in Tolkien, *Tree and Leaf*, 4.

7   Quoted in Humphrey Carpenter, *The Inklings* (London: Allen & Unwin, 1978), 57.

8   *Letters of C. S. Lewis*, ed. W. H. Lewis (London: Geoffrey Bles, 1966), 287. The word *bandersnatch*, invented by Lewis Carroll, and also used by Lewis in his *Allegory of Love*, is defined thus by the *OED*: "A fleet, furious, fuming, fabulous creature, of dangerous propensities, immune to bribery and too fast to flee from; later, used vaguely to suggest any creature with such qualities."

9   Carpenter, *The Inklings*, 42. N.b. A considerable amount has been written on Barfield's influence on Lewis, but much less on his influence on Tolkien. I am aware of no one who has made any connection to *History in English Words*, though there *must* be others who have noted the direct influence of its content upon Tolkien.

10 Carpenter, *The Inklings*, 41.

11 With thanks to Humphrey Carpenter for the illustration. While German philosopher Ernst Cassirer put forth a similar argument, it appears that the two men developed their theories independently, if contemporaneously; *The Inklings*, 42. Cassirer's treatment of mythopoeic thought as a legitimate form of knowledge, made available in English in the 1950s, was significant in the direction of philosophical understanding of knowledge acquisition and influenced the work of scholars such as the Frankforts and Slochower.

12 Carpenter, *The Inklings*, 42.

13 Owen Barfield, *History in English Words* (London: Faber & Faber, 1926), 83.

14 J. R. R. Tolkien, *The Lord of the Rings*, Single volume anniversary ed. (London: HarperCollins, 2005), 80.

15 Barfield, *History in English Words*, 188–90.
16 Tolkien, *Tree and Leaf*, 67.
17 Barfield, *History in English Words*, 189.
18 Barfield, *History in English Words*, 190. Barfield is referencing Elizabethan critic George Puttenham, from *The Art of English Poesy*, 1589.
19 Barfield, *History in English Words*, 190.
20 Barfield, *History in English Words*, 190.
21 "On Fairy-Stories," 73.
22 *Letters of J. R. R. Tolkien*, 145 [131, undated, to Milton Waldman].
23 Barfield, *History in English Words*, 196.
24 C. S. Lewis, *Collected Letters*, ed. Walter Hooper, vol. 1 (San Francisco: HarperCollins, 1931), 967–68 [18 October 1931, to Arthur Greeves], first emphasis mine. As the word *myth* can be a "red flag" to many different camps, and in common discourse has devolved to insinuate something false, it is important to pay close attention to Lewis's words here: "a true myth," something that "really happened." Lewis addresses this at length in his essay "Myth Became Fact." The paragraph following will reiterate Lewis and Tolkien's understanding of what a *myth* is.
25 Carpenter, *The Inklings*, 43.
26 Carpenter, *The Inklings*, 43.
27 This particular phrasing is found in C. S. Lewis's letters, 22 September 1956; emphasis mine.
28 "Myth Became Fact," in C. S. Lewis, "Myth Became Fact," *God in the Dock* (Glasgow: William Collins & Son, 1955), 43.
29 *God in the Dock*, 44. To quote Lewis here more thoroughly:

"The heart of Christianity is a myth which is also a fact. The old myth of the Dying God, *without ceasing to be myth*, comes down from the heaven of legend and imagination to the earth of history. It *happens*—at a particular date, in a particular place, followed by definable historical consequences. We pass from a Balder or an Osiris, dying nobody knows when or where, to a historical Person crucified (it is all in order) *under Pontius Pilate*. By becoming fact it does not cease to be myth: that is the miracle. I suspect that men have sometimes derived more spiritual sustenance from myths they did not believe than from the religion they professed. To be truly Christian we must both assent to the historical fact and also receive the myth (fact though it has become) with the same imaginative embrace which we accord to all myth. The one is hardly more necessary than the other."

30 "In our world," said Eustace, "a star is a huge ball of flaming gas." "Even
   in your world, my son, that is not what a star is but only what it is made of
   . . . ." from "Mythopoeia" in Tolkien, *Tree and Leaf*, 85, 87.
31 Carpenter, *The Inklings*, 44; italics mine.
32 Carpenter, *The Inklings*, 45.
33 Tolkien, *Tree and Leaf*, 88–89.
34 C. S. Lewis, *Of This and Other Worlds* (Glasgow: William Collins, 1955),
   61.
35 *Letters of C. S. Lewis*, 271.
36 This distinction is of immense significance, for misinterpretation has
   led many Lewis scholars, let alone Lewis devotees, to underestimate the
   incredible depth to which Lewis—and Lewis's writing—is shaped by this
   man whom he calls his "spiritual mentor."
37 George MacDonald, *An Anthology*, ed. C. S. Lewis (London: Geoffrey
   Bles, 1970), xxviii. Levy-Bruhl explores this when he points out the distinction that, while a poem is untranslatable, a mythical narrative can be
   translated into any language.
38 MacDonald, *An Anthology*, x.
39 Lewis, *Of This and Other Worlds*, 25.
40 MacDonald, *An Anthology*, xviii.
41 Tolkien, *Tree and Leaf*, 53.
42 Stratford Caldecott, *Secret Fire: The Spiritual Vision of J. R. R. Tolkien* (London:
   Dartman, Longman & Todd, 2003), 1.
43 *Letters of J. R. R. Tolkien*, 310 [234, 22 November 1961, to Jane Neave].
44 *Letters of J. R. R. Tolkien*, 153 [130, 14 September 1950, from a letter to Sir
   Stanley Unwin].
45 Tolkien, *The Lord of the Rings*, 240, cf. 764.
46 Tolkien, *The Lord of the Rings*; see, e.g., 251–54.
47 Tolkien, *The Lord of the Rings*, 374.
48 Tolkien, *The Lord of the Rings*, 865.
49 Tolkien had read the lay to Lewis in the early days of their friendship—
   leading to Lewis's enthusiastic letter to Greeves, quoted earlier.
50 Tolkien, *The Lord of the Rings*, 1056, Appendix A.
51 Faramir opines in sorrow to Frodo that "Gondor men can no longer call
   themselves High" because they now hold skill of battle in greater esteem
   than other crafts and knowledge. *The Lord of the Rings*, 679.
52 Tolkien, *The Lord of the Rings*, 669; italics mine.
53 Tolkien, *The Lord of the Rings*, 681.
54 Tolkien, *The Lord of the Rings*, 694.

55 Tolkien, *The Lord of the Rings*, 549–50.
56 Tolkien, *The Lord of the Rings*, 247.
57 Tolkien, *The Lord of the Rings*, 711–13. The concept of "branches on the Tree of Tales," an image from "On Fairy-Stories," is explored further in Tolkien's story "Leaf by Niggle."
58 *Letters of J. R. R. Tolkien*, 110 [96, 30 January 1945, to Christopher Tolkien]. Christopher was at that time serving overseas during WWII.
59 Tolkien, *The Lord of the Rings*, 1029.
60 Deuteronomy 4:9; 11:19.
61 Letter to Katherine Farrer, quoted in Carpenter, *The Inklings*, 160.

Chapter 4

1 From the essay "On Fairy-Stories," in Tolkien, *Tree and Leaf*, 55.
2 See J. R. R. Tolkien, *"The Monsters and the Critics" and Other Essays* (London: HarperCollins, 1997).
3 I.e., not just *The Lord of the Rings*, but the wider, vast literary "world" within which this tale was situated, which itself was as yet, of course, unpublished. See *Letters of J. R. R. Tolkien*, 188 [153, draft, to Peter Hastings]. The letter was apparently never sent, but its contents offer an illuminating, the way in which Tolkien remained exercised by the issues he had addressed in St. Andrews in March 1939. A related suggestion is contained in an earlier letter to Milton Waldman written in 1951: "all this stuff," Tolkien writes (alluding to his entire mythological enterprise), "is mainly concerned with Fall, Mortality, and the Machine" (*Letters of J. R. R. Tolkien*, 145 [131, undated, to Milton Waldman]). A footnote to the text reads: "It is, I suppose, fundamentally concerned with the problem of the relation of Art (and Sub-creation) and Primary Reality."
4 Tolkien does not, of course, suggest that his thinking on the subject underwent no significant development over the years, though it must be admitted that it seems to have remained more or less constant as far as the basic shape and significance of the essential idea is concerned.
5 Cited in Nicholas Wolterstorff, *Art in Action: Toward a Christian Aesthetic* (Carlisle: Solway, 1997).
6 See Caldecott, *Secret Fire*, 73.
7 Ralph C. Wood, *The Gospel According to Tolkien: Visions of the Kingdom in Middle-earth* (Louisville: Westminster John Knox, 2003).
8 See, e.g., Tolkien, *"The Monsters and the Critics" and Other Essays*, 7, and Tolkien, *Tree and Leaf*, 23f. In 1947 Tolkien agreed to let Rayner Unwin, the (now adult) son of the publisher Sir Stanley Unwin, see his complete

draft of the first part of *The Lord of the Rings*. (Ten years earlier, as a young boy, Rayner had served as the guinea pig on whom the draft of *The Hobbit* had been tested with great success.) In July 1947, in response to Rayner's reported comments on the draft, Tolkien writes: ". . . do not let Rayner suspect 'Allegory.' There is a 'moral,' I suppose, in any tale worth telling. But that is not the same thing" (*Letters of J. R. R. Tolkien*, 121 [109, 31 July 1947, to Sir Stanley Unwin]). In the 1951 letter to Milton Waldman cited above he reiterates the point: "I dislike Allegory—the conscious and intentional allegory—yet any attempt to explain the purport of myth or fairytale must use allegorical language" (*Letters of J. R. R. Tolkien*, 145 [131, undated, to Milton Waldman]). Despite such vigorous avowals of dislike, though, Tolkien did himself occasionally lean in the direction of allegory. He does so quite explicitly, for instance, in the essay "Beowulf: The Monsters and the Critics," with his parable of the tower (see *"The Monsters and the Critics," and Other Essays*, 7f.). And, while less explicit, it is hard to resist Shippey's insistence that the story "Leaf by Niggle" (1943) "certainly is" an allegory, seemingly being about Tolkien's own inability to get *The Lord of the Rings* written (because of his endless "niggling" over minutiae), its impact on his more strictly professional work, and the likelihood that he might not complete it before his death; see Tom Shippey, *The Road to Middle-earth: How J. R. R. Tolkien Created a New Mythology*, rev. and exp. ed. (London: HarperCollins, 2005), 50f. Cf. Tolkien, *"The Monsters and the Critics," and Other Essays*, 260f. Oddly, Tolkien mentions "Leaf by Niggle" in one of the very letters disdaining allegory, yet fails to draw any link between the two topics! See *Letters of J. R. R. Tolkien*, 145 [131, undated (1951), to Milton Waldman].

9 So, for instance: "A fairytale is not an allegory. There may be allegory in it, but it is not an allegory. He must be an artist indeed who can, in any mode, produce a strict allegory that is not a weariness to the spirit. An allegory must be Mastery or Moorditch" (George MacDonald, *A Dish of Orts: Chiefly Papers on the Imagination and on Shakespeare* [London: Sampson Low Marston, 1893], 317).

10 *Letters of J. R. R. Tolkien*, 145 [131, undated (1951), to Milton Waldman] and 121 [109, 31 July 1947, to Sir Stanley Unwin].

11 *Letters of J. R. R. Tolkien*, 121 [109, 31 July 1947, to Sir Stanley Unwin].

12 *Letters of J. R. R. Tolkien*, 121 [109, 31 July 1947, to Sir Stanley Unwin].

13 Caldecott, 74.

14 Shippey, *Road to Middle-earth*, 267. The description pertains to *The Silmarillion* as a whole, but in the relevant paragraph Shippey expounds it in relation to "Ainulindalë" in particular.

15 So, for example: "Nothing even remotely polytheistic is suggested here."
    Wood, 12.

16 *Letters of J. R. R. Tolkien*, 191 [153, undated draft (1954), to Peter Hastings].

17 The key dramatic motif in *The Lord of the Rings*, he suggested later, is "not
    'freedom,' though that is naturally involved. It is about God, and His sole
    right to divine honour" (*Letters of J. R. R. Tolkien*, 243 [undated (1956), Notes
    on W. H. Auden's review of *The Return of the King*]. Tolkien's commitments
    here echo George MacDonald's insistence that "The laws of the spirit of
    man must hold, alike in this world and in any world he may invent. . . . In
    physical things a man may invent; in moral things he must obey—and take
    their laws with him into his invented world as well" (*Dish of Orts*, 316).

18 J. R. R. Tolkien, *The Silmarillion* (London: HarperCollins, 1992), 3.

19 Tolkien, *The Silmarillion*, 15.

20 Tolkien, *The Silmarillion*, 4.

21 "Crown Him with Many Crowns" by Matthew Bridges (1800–1894) and
    Godfrey Thring (1823–1903). The full text may be found in *The Methodist
    Hymn-Book* (London: Methodist Conference Office, 1933), No. 271.

22 It is Melkor, in fact, who in the myth seeks in vain to obliterate God's
    music by turning up the volume. Thus, his music "was loud and . . . end-
    lessly repeated; and it had little harmony, but rather a clamorous unison
    as of many trumpets braying upon a few notes. And it essayed to drown
    the other music by the violence of its voice, but it seemed that its most
    triumphant notes were taken by the other and woven into its own solemn
    pattern." Tolkien, *The Silmarillion*, 5.

23 Tolkien, *The Silmarillion*, 5–6.

24 Christian theology, too, of course, has always had to reckon with the fact
    that, to the extent that God is sovereign, the presence of evil and suffer-
    ing in the world he has made must, ultimately, be something for which he
    bears some form and level of responsibility, even though he cannot be sup-
    posed to be its immediate author.

25 Tolkien, *The Silmarillion*, 9. This is a departure from some earlier recensions
    of the text (see further below) in which the world's creation and the sing-
    ing and playing of the Ainur are apparently more immediately linked.

26 Tolkien, *Tree and Leaf*, 30.

27 Shippey, *Road to Middle-earth*, 56f.

28 For an account of this period (autumn 1918–summer 1920), see Carpenter,
    A Biography, 139ff.

29 *Letters of J. R. R. Tolkien*, 345 [257, 16 July 1964, to Christopher Bretherton].
    Although the recollection straddles some forty-five years, Christopher

Tolkien observes that there is no evidence to set against it. See J. R. R. Tolkien, *The Book of Lost Tales, Part 1*, ed. Christopher Tolkien (London: HarperCollins, 1992), 45. For the text of "The Music of the Ainur" see 52–63.

30 Christopher Tolkien identifies four key stages in the development: (i) the early version dating from c. 1919; (ii) a revision (version B) dating from the late 1930s, immediately prior to the preparation and delivery of the Andrew Lang Lecture; (iii) a further revision (version C) carried out in the mid-late 1940s; (iv) the final revision (version D), dating from the early 1950s. See on this J. R. R. Tolkien, *Morgoth's Ring*, ed. Christopher Tolkien (London: HarperCollins, 1993), 3–44. Although Christopher Tolkien suggests that some of the revisions were "drastic," and had to do with some seismic shifts in Tolkien's imaginary cosmology itself (see, e.g., 3), for our purposes the elements of essential continuity are far more significant.

31 Tolkien, *Book of Lost Tales, Part 1*, 53.

32 *Letters of J. R. R. Tolkien*, 188 [153, draft, to Peter Hastings], 145 [131, undated, to Milton Waldman].

33 Tolkien, *Book of Lost Tales, Part 1*, 53.

34 Christopher Tolkien suggests that this new version was produced by following the text of the original very closely and rephrasing it as needed, a process Tolkien seems not to have followed in his reworking of others among the "Lost Tales." Tolkien, *Lost Road and Other Writings*, 155.

35 Tolkien, *Lost Road and Other Writings*, 156.

36 The so-called "version C" produced in the 1940s. See Tolkien, *Morgoth's Ring*, 3ff.

37 See Tolkien, *Morgoth's Ring*, 8, 13.

38 Tolkien, *Morgoth's Ring*, 25.

39 *Letters of J. R. R. Tolkien*, 145 [131, undated (1951), to Milton Waldman].

40 Years later Tolkien himself would interpret his mythology in terms of the categories of "On Fairy-Stories." Thus, for example: "The Ainur took part in the making of the world as "sub-creators." . . . They interpreted according to their powers, and completed in detail, the Design propounded to them by the One"; *Letters of J. R. R. Tolkien*, 284 [212, undated draft (October 1948) to Rhona Beare]. It is interesting to note that, having the category of "sub-creator" clearly in place, the language of "completion" no longer risks misunderstanding and is freely deployed.

41 Strictly, they must be supposed to have some form of existence in the imaginative vision itself, but they are not yet "real" in the full-blooded sense of there being a world in which they are the case.

42 Tolkien, *Tree and Leaf*, 23.

43 Tolkien, *Tree and Leaf*, 48.

44 *Letters of J. R. R. Tolkien*, 188 [153, undated draft (1954), to Peter Hastings].

45 The sort of imaginative meddling that, no matter how cleverly done, alters the world in order to secure power over it, to dominate things and wills, Tolkien calls "magic." See, e.g., Tolkien, *Tree and Leaf*, 53.

46 Tolkien, *Tree and Leaf*, 50.

47 *Letters of J. R. R. Tolkien*, 412 [328, undated draft (Autumn 1971) to Caroline Batten-Phelps].

Chapter 5

1 Andrew Lang, "Preface," *The Maid of France* (Longmans, Green, 1913), v.

2 Tolkien, *Tree and Leaf*, 4.

3 Tolkien, *Tree and Leaf*, 11.

4 Tolkien, *Tree and Leaf*, 14.

5 Tolkien, *Tree and Leaf*, 6.

6 Tolkien, *Tree and Leaf*, 49–52.

7 Tolkien, *Tree and Leaf*, 68.

8 Tolkien, *Tree and Leaf*, 68.

9 Tolkien, *Tree and Leaf*, 50.

10 Tolkien, *Tree and Leaf*, 52.

11 Tolkien, *Tree and Leaf*, 69.

12 Tolkien, *Tree and Leaf*, 69.

13 Christopher Marlowe, *Marlow's Doctor Faustus: 1604–1616*, ed. W. W. Greg (Oxford: Claredon, 1950), 269–70.

14 Marlowe, 166.

15 Marlowe, 166.

16 Jean-Paul Sartre, "No Exit," in *No Exit and Three Other Plays*, trans. Stuart Gilbert (New York: Vintage International, 1989), 45.

17 Marlowe, 180.

18 "Books" in François M. A. de Voltaire, *Dictionnaire Philosophique* (Paris, 1764).

19 Henry David Thoreau, *Walden* (Columbus, Ohio: Charles E. Merrill, 1969), 110.

20 Matthew Arnold, "The Study of Poetry, Second Series," in *Essays in Criticism* (London: Macmillan, 1908), 2.

21 Arnold, 21.

22 James Joyce, A *Portrait of the Artist as a Young Man* (London: Jonathan Cape, 1942), 244.

23 Bernard Williams, *Truth and Truthfulness: An Essay in Genealogy* (Princeton: Princeton University Press, 2002), 8.

24 Friedrich Nietzsche, *The Birth of Tragedy and Other Writings*, ed. Raymond Geuss and Ronald Speirs, trans. Ronald Speirs (Cambridge: Cambridge University Press, 1999), 41.

25 Arnold, 21–22.

26 Williams, 3.

27 Williams, 49.

28 Williams, 57.

29 David Lyle Jeffrey, *People of the Book* (Grand Rapids: Eerdmans, Institute for Advanced Christian Studies, 1996). David Lyle Jeffrey, *Houses of the Interpreter: Reading Scripture, Reading Culture* (Waco, Tex.: Baylor University Press, 2003).

30 David Aikman, *Jesus in Beijing: How Christianity Is Transforming China and Changing the Global Balance of Power* (Washington, D.C.: Regnery, 2003), 254.

31 Williams, 262–63.

32 George Steiner, "To Civilize Our Gentlemen," in *Language and Silence: Essays on Language, Literature, and the Inhuman* (New Haven: Yale University Press, 1998), 62.

33 Terry Eagleton, *After Theory* (New York: Basic Books, 2003), 2–3.

34 Eagleton, 29.

35 George Steiner, *Real Presences* (Chicago: The University of Chicago Press, 1989), 143.

36 Steiner, *Real Presences*, 55.

37 Williams, 103, 105.

38 "Hence poetry is something more philosophic and of graver import than history, since its statements are of the nature rather of universals, whereas those of history are singulars." Aristotle, *Poetics*. In *Aristotle's Poetics: Longinus on the Sublime*, ed. Charles Sears (1930), 18. Cf. William Wordsworth, *Lyrical Ballads, with Other Poems* (Philadelphia: James Humphreys, 1802).

39 Williams, 8.

40 Marlowe, 290.

41 J. Budziszewski, *What We Can't Not Know: A Guide* (Dallas: Spence Publishing, 2003), 19.

42 Williams, 45.

43 Marlowe, 277.

44 Jacques Maritain, "The Frontiers of Poetry," in *Art and Scholasticism with Other Essays*, trans. J. F. Scanlan (New York: Charles Scribner's Sons, 1942), 101.

Chapter 6

1   The title of the paper on which this chapter is based was "Unheroic Gardeners: The Necessary Failure in *The Lord of the Rings* films." The paper was delivered on 8 March 2004.

2   *Letters of J. R. R. Tolkien*, 261 [202, 11 September 1957, from a letter to Christopher and Faith Tolkien].

3   *Letters of J. R. R. Tolkien*, 272 [210, undated (June 1958), from a letter to Forrest J. Ackerman].

4   *Letters of J. R. R. Tolkien*, 277 [210, undated (June 1958), from a letter to Forrest J. Ackerman].

5   *Letters of J. R. R. Tolkien*, 270 [210, undated (June 1958), from a letter to Forrest J. Ackerman].

6   Ursula K. Le Guin, "The Carrier Bag Theory of Fiction," in *Dancing at the Edge of the World: Thoughts on Words, Women, Places* (New York: Harper & Row, 1989), 165.

7   Le Guin, 165.

8   Le Guin, 165–66.

9   Tolkien, *The Lord of the Rings*, 711–12.

10 Le Guin, 166–67.

11 Le Guin, 168.

12 Le Guin, 169.

13 Le Guin, 168–69.

14 Tolkien, *The Lord of the Rings*, 475–76.

15 Tolkien, *The Lord of the Rings*, 650.

16 Tolkien, *The Lord of the Rings*, 681.

17 Tolkien, *The Lord of the Rings*, 681.

18 Tolkien, *The Lord of the Rings*, 965.

19 Tolkien, *The Lord of the Rings*, 375.

20 Tolkien, *The Lord of the Rings*, 758.

21 Tolkien, *Tree and Leaf*, 72–73.

Chapter 7

1   That Tolkien's epic offers such an echo of Christian faith is the argument I make in Wood, *Gospel According to Tolkien*.

2   John Garth, *Tolkien and the Great War: The Threshold of Middle-earth* (Boston: Houghton Mifflin, 2003).

3   Shippey, *Road to Middle-earth*, 370n14.

4   Shippey, *Author of the Century*, 133.

5   Shippey, *Author of the Century*, 134.

6   Verlyn Flieger offers precisely such a Jungian reading of Tolkien, arguing that the Ring story represents the equally balanced opposites of light and darkness, good and evil, within every person; cf. Verlyn Flieger, *Splintered Light: Logos and Language in Tolkien's World* (Grand Rapids: Eerdmans, 1983).

7   G. R. Evans, *Augustine on Evil* (Cambridge: Cambridge University Press, 1994), 14.

8   Evans, 5.

9   Augustine, *Saint Augustine: Confessions*, trans. Henry Chadwick (Oxford: Oxford University Press, 1992), III, vii, 43.

10   Evans, 3.

11   Tolkien, *The Lord of the Rings*, 32.

12   Tolkien, *The Lord of the Rings*, 945.

13   The power of sin to enslave the will is poignantly described by St. Paul in the epistle to the Romans: "For what I am doing, I do not understand . . . for the willing is present in me, but the doing of the good is not. For the good that I want, I do not do, but I practice the very evil that I do not want. But if I am doing the very thing I do not want, I am no longer the one doing it, but sin which dwells in me. . . . Wretched man that I am! Who will set me free from the body of this death?" (Rom 7:15a, 18b–20, 24).

14   Tolkien, *The Lord of the Rings*, 919, 938.

15   John Howard Yoder cites the Tower of Babel story in Genesis 11 as an argument against any hegemonic universalism. Rather than reading the destruction of Babel merely as God's angry reprimand, he sees it also as a benevolent divine corrective to an arrogant attempt at an imperially enforced uniformity. The Babylonians "were the first foundationalists," Yoder writes, seeking to overcome all historically developing diversity by recourse to their own cultural power. The "confusion" of tongues at Babel is thus God's gracious intervention to continue the process of dispersion and diversification whereby we are meant to learn humility through respect for the other. "It is not a punishment or tragedy," Yoder concludes, "but the gift of new beginnings, liberation from a blind alley." *For the Nations: Essays Evangelical and Public* (Grand Rapids: Eerdmans, 1997), 63.

16   Not for Tolkien, it follows, the Enlightenment-inspired dream of transcending locality for the sake of putatively universal values. He lived long

enough, alas, to witness the slaughter of roughly 180 million human beings in the name of supposedly timeless and placeless truths. As a Christian, Tolkien takes his stand on the *terra firma* of English language and climate, retrieving from other cultures and literatures those virtues which were congruent with his faith. Yet he abominated the prospect of English emerging as the new *lingua franca* of the commercial world. Such a commodifying of his native tongue would destroy the vitality of the many local languages that English would come to displace, Tolkien complained, while also ruining the rich local dialects of English itself. Such cultural and linguistic pluralism prevents Tolkien's imaginative metanarrative enterprise from becoming triumphalist.

17 In fairness, it should be noted that Shippey regards this allegedly dual conception of evil as a virtue rather than a vice: "One has to say that this is one of the work's great strengths. We all recognize, in our better moments at least, that much harm comes from our own imperfections, sometimes terribly magnified, like traffic deaths from haste and aggression and reluctance to leave the party too soon: those are temptations. At the same time there are other disasters for which one feels no responsibility at all, like (as Tolkien was writing) bombs and gas chambers." *Author of the Century*, 142. On the contrary, Christian teaching holds that earthquakes and typhoons and bodily deformities are the only things for which we "have no responsibility at all." When asked whether it was the man who was blind from birth or his parents who had sinned, Jesus replied that neither was at fault (John 9:2-3). We *are* responsible for bombs and gas chambers, since they are the works of fellow creatures whose sin, in taking these sinister forms, differs from ours only in degree, not in kind. Hence the celebrated saying of Father Zossima in *The Brothers Karamazov*: "All are responsible for all."

18 Tolkien, *The Lord of the Rings*, 1018.

19 "The Church and the Sacraments," in *The Cambridge Companion to Christian Doctrine*, ed. Colin E. Gunton (Cambridge: Cambridge University Press, 1997), 210.

20 Shippey, *Road to Middle-earth*, 153.

21 Tolkien, *The Lord of the Rings*, 276.

22 Tolkien, *The Lord of the Rings*, 105.

23 Tolkien, *The Silmarillion*, 108, emphasis added.

24 Tolkien, *The Lord of the Rings*, 922.

25 Tolkien, *The Lord of the Rings*, 59.

26 Tolkien, *The Lord of the Rings*, 713.

BIBLIOGRAPHY

Aikman, David. *Jesus in Beijing: How Christianity Is Transforming China and Changing the Global Balance of Power.* Washington, D.C.: Regnery, 2003.

Alderson, Brian, *The Hobbit, 50th Anniversary.* Oxford: Unwin Hyman, 1987.

— — —, ed. *Red Fairy Book, Collected by Andrew Lang.* Harmondsworth: Kestrel, 1976.

Anon. *The St. Andrews Citizen,* 11 March 1939.

Aristotle. *Poetics.* In *Aristotle's Poetics: Longinus on the Sublime.* Edited by Charles Sears. New York: Macmillan, 1930. 3–53.

Arnold, Matthew. "The Study of Poetry, Second Series." *Essays in Criticism.* London: Macmillan, 1908. 1–55.

Augustine. *Saint Augustine: Confessions.* Translated by Henry Chadwick. Oxford: Oxford University Press, 1992.

Barfield, Owen. *History in English Words.* London: Faber & Faber, 1926.

— — —. *Poetic Diction: A Study in Meaning.* 2nd ed. London: Faber & Faber, 1962.

Budziszewski, J. *What We Can't Not Know: A Guide.* Dallas: Spence Publishing, 2003.

Caldecott, Stratford. *Secret Fire: The Spiritual Vision of J. R. R. Tolkien.* London: Dartman, Longman & Todd, 2003.

Carpenter, Humphrey. *The Inklings.* London: Allen & Unwin, 1978.

———. *J. R. R. Tolkien: A Biography.* London: HarperCollins, 2002.

Day, David, and Lidia Postma (illustrator). *The Hobbit Companion.* London: Pavillion Books, 2002.

Eagleton, Terry. *After Theory.* New York: Basic Books, 2003.

Evans, G. R. *Augustine on Evil.* Cambridge: Cambridge University Press, 1994.

Fergusson, James. *Shakespeare's Scotland: being the Andrew Lang lecture delivered before the University of St. Andrews, 14 November 1956.* Edinburgh: Thomas Nelson & Sons, 1957.

Flieger, Verlyn. *Splintered Light: Logos and Language in Tolkien's World.* Grand Rapids: Eerdmans, 1983.

Garth, John. *Tolkien and the Great War: The Threshold of Middle-Earth.* Boston: Houghton Mifflin, 2003.

Green, Roger Lancelyn. "Andrew Lang and the Fairy Tale." *Review of English Studies* 20 (1944): 227–31.

Green, William H. *The Hobbit: A Journey into Maturity.* New York: Twayne Publishers, 1995.

Gunton, Colin E., ed. *The Cambridge Companion to Christian Doctrine.* Cambridge: Cambridge University Press, 1997.

Hammond, Wayne G. and Douglas Anderson (assistant). *J. R. R. Tolkien: A Descriptive Bibliography.* Winchester: St. Paul's Bibliographies, 1993.

Hammond, Wayne G., and Christina Scull. *J. R. R. Tolkien: Artist and Illustrator.* London: HarperCollins, 1995.

Helms, Randel. *Tolkien's World.* London: Houghton Mifflin, 1974.

Houfe, Simon. *The Dictionary of British Book Illustrators and Caricaturists 1800–1914.* Woodbridge: Baron Publishing, 1978.

Jeffrey, David Lyle. *Houses of the Interpreter: Reading Scripture, Reading Culture.* Waco, Tex.: Baylor University Press, 2003.

———. *People of the Book.* Grand Rapids: Eerdmans, Institute for Advanced Christian Studies, 1996.

Joyce, James. *A Portrait of the Artist as a Young Man.* London: Jonathan Cape, 1942.

Lang, Andrew. *Red Fairy Book*. London: Longmans, Green, 1890.

— — —. "Preface." *The Maid of France*. 1908. London: Longmans, Green, 1913.

Le Guin, Ursula K. "The Carrier Bag Theory of Fiction." *Dancing at the Edge of the World: Thoughts on Words, Women, Places*. New York: Harper & Row, 1989.

Lewis, C. S. *Collected Letters*. Vol. 1. Edited by Walter Hooper. San Francisco: HarperCollins, 1931.

— — —, ed. *Essays Presented to Charles Williams*. London: Oxford University Press, 1947.

— — —. *Letters of C. S. Lewis*. Edited by W. H. Lewis. London: Geoffrey Bles, 1966.

— — —. "Myth Became Fact." *God in the Dock*. Glasgow: William Collins & Son, 1955.

— — —. *Of This and Other Worlds*. Glasgow: William Collins & Son, 1955.

— — —. *Rehabilitations and Other Essays*. London: Oxford University Press, 1939.

MacDonald, George. *An Anthology*. Edited by C. S. Lewis. London: Geoffrey Bles, 1970.

— — —. *A Dish of Orts: Chiefly Papers on the Imagination and on Shakespeare*. London: Sampson Low Marston, 1893.

Macmillan, Baron Hugh Pattison. *Law and Custom: being the Andrew Lang lecture delivered before the University of St. Andrews, 5 April 1948*. Edinburgh: Nelson & Sons, 1949.

Manlove, Colin. *Christian Fantasy: From 1200 to the Present*. Notre Dame, Ind.: University of Notre Dame Press, 1992.

Maritain, Jacques. *Art and Scholasticism with Other Essays*. Translated by J. F. Scanlan. New York: Charles Scribner's Sons, 1942..

Marlowe, Christopher. *Marlowe's Doctor Faustus: 1604–1616*. Edited by W. W. Greg. Oxford: Clarendon, 1950.

Murray, Gilbert. *Andrew Lang the poet: being the Andrew Lang lecture delivered before the University of St. Andrews, 7 May 1947*. London: Oxford University Press, 1948.

Nietzsche, Friedrich. *The Birth of Tragedy and Other Writings*. Edited by Raymond Geuss and Ronald Speirs. Translated by Ronald Speirs. Cambridge: Cambridge University Press, 1999.

Owen, Meic Pierce. "Tolkien and St. Andrews." *University of St. Andrews Staff Newsletter*, January 2004.

Rosebury, Brian. *J. R. R. Tolkien: A Critical Assessment*. Basingstoke: Macmillan, 1992.

Ryan, J. S. "Two Oxford Scholars' Perceptions of the Traditional Germanic Hall." *Minas Tirith Evening-Star* 19 (1990): 8–11.

Sartre, Jean-Paul. *No Exit and Three Other Plays*. Translated by Stuart Gilbert. New York: Vintage International, 1989.

Scull, Christina. "Dragons from Andrews Lang's Retelling of Sigurd to Tolkien's Chrysophylax." In *Leaves from the Tree: J. R. R. Tolkien's Shorter Fiction*. London: The Tolkien Society, 1991.

Sears, Charles, ed. *Aristotle's Poetics: Longinus on the Sublime*. Edited by Charles Sears. New York: Macmillan, 1930.

Shippey, T. A. *J. R. R. Tolkien: Author of the Century*. Boston: Houghton Mifflin, 2001.

———. *The Road to Middle-earth: How J. R. R. Tolkien Created a New Mythology*. Revised and expanded. London: HarperCollins, 2005.

Steiner, George. *Real Presences*. Chicago: University of Chicago Press, 1989.

———. "To Civilize Our Gentlemen." In *Language and Silence: Essays on Language, Literature, and the Inhuman*. New Haven: Yale University Press, 1998. 55–67.

Thoreau, Henry David. *Walden*. Columbus, Ohio: Charles E. Merrill Publishing, 1969.

Tillyard, E. M. W., and C. S. Lewis. *The Personal Heresy: A Controversy*. Oxford: Oxford University Press, 1965.

Tolkien, Christopher. *Pictures by J. R. R. Tolkien*. London: HarperCollins, 1992.

Tolkien, J. R. R. *The Book of Lost Tales, Part 1*. Edited by Christopher Tolkien. London: HarperCollins, 1992.

———. Letter to Professor T. Malcolm Knox. University of St. Andrews Library, ms37525/512.

———. *The Letters of J. R. R. Tolkien*. Edited by Humphrey Carpenter. London: HarperCollins, 1999.

———. *The Lord of the Rings*. Single volume anniversary edition. London: HarperCollins, 2005.

———. *The Lost Road and Other Writings*. Edited by Christopher Tolkien. London: HarperCollins, 1992.

———. *"The Monsters and the Critics" and Other Essays*. London: HarperCollins, 1997.

———. *Morgoth's Ring*. Edited by Christopher Tolkien. London: HarperCollins, 1993.

———. "On Fairy-Stories." In *Essays Presented to Charles Williams*. Edited by C. S. Lewis. London: Oxford University Press, 1947. 38–89.

———. *The Silmarillion*. London: HarperCollins, 1992.

———. *Tree and Leaf: Including the Poem Mythopoeia, the Homecoming of Beorhtnoth Beorhthelm's Son*. London: HarperCollins, 2001.

Voltaire, François M.A. de. *Dictionnaire Philosophique*. Paris, 1764.

Vredenburg, Edric. *The Fairy Tale Book*. London: Raphael Tuck & Sons, 1920.

Watson, Victor, ed. *The Cambridge Guide to Children's Books in English*. Cambridge: Cambridge University Press, 2001.

Webster, A. Blyth and J. B. Salmond, eds. *Concerning Andrew Lang: Being the Andrew Lang Lectures Delivered before the University of St. Andrews, 1927–1937*. Oxford: Clarendon, 1949.

White, Michael. *Tolkien: A Biography*. London: Abacus, 2002.

Williams, Bernard. *Truth and Truthfulness: An Essay in Genealogy*. Princeton: Princeton University Press, 2002.

Wolterstorff, Nicholas. *Art in Action: Toward a Christian Aesthetic*. Carlisle: Solway, 1997.

Wood, Ralph C. *The Gospel According to Tolkien: Visions of the Kingdom in Middle-earth*. Louisville: Westminster John Knox, 2003.

Wordsworth, William. *Lyrical Ballads, with Other Poems*. Philadelphia: James Humphreys, 1802.

Yoder, John Howard. *For the Nations: Essays Evangelical and Public*. Grand Rapids: Eerdmans, 1997.

ABOUT THE CONTRIBUTORS

COLIN DURIEZ is a freelance writer based in Cumbria with several Tolkien and Lewis related publications to his credit.

RACHEL HART is muniments archivist in the Department of Special Collections, University of St. Andrews Library.

TREVOR HART is professor of divinity and director of the Institute for Theology, Imagination and the Arts, University of St. Andrews.

DAVID LYLE JEFFREY is distinguished professor of literature and the humanities, Baylor University, Waco, Texas.

KIRSTIN JOHNSON is a research student in the Institute for Theology, Imagination and the Arts, University of St. Andrews.

IVAN KHOVACS is a research student in the Institute for Theology, Imagination and the Arts, University of St. Andrews.

LOREN WILKINSON is professor of interdisciplinary studies at Regent College, Vancouver, BC.

RALPH WOOD is university professor of theology and literature, Baylor University, Waco, Texas.

INDEX

Ackermann, Forrest J., 117
Addison, Joseph, 29
Aeschylus, 57, 67
Aikman, David, 116
Alderson, Brian, 10, 106
allegory, 17, 41, 42, 56, 112
Anderson, Douglas, 105
Aragorn, 35, 36, 75, 82, 97
Aristotle, 64, 102, 116
Arnold, Matthew, 62, 63, 64, 68, 115
Arnold, Thomas, 61–62
art, 50, 52, 53, 111
Auden, W. H., 25, 106, 113
Augustine, 86, 87, 88, 90, 94, 95, 118

Baggins, Bilbo, 9
Baggins, Frodo, 35, 37, 75, 79, 85, 91,
    92, 93, 94, 97, 98, 99, 100, 101, 110
Barfield, Owen, 18, 27, 28, 29, 30, 31,
    33, 108; History in English Words, 27,
    28, 108, 109; Poetic Diction, 20, 27,
    107
Barth, Karl, 87

Batten-Phelps, Caroline, 115
Baynes, Pauline, 104
Beare, Rhona, 114
Bennett, Andrew, 103
Boethius, 86
Boromir, 35, 36, 80, 82, 97
Bradley, A. C., 57
Bretherton, Christopher, 113
Bridges, Matthew, 113
Budziszewski, J., 116
Bunyan, John, 34

Caldecott, Stratford, 34, 42, 43, 110,
    111, 112
Campbell, Joseph, 73
Carpenter, Humphrey, 3, 11, 72,
    108; The Inklings, 108, 109, 110, 111;
    J.R.R. Tolkien: A Biography, 104, 105,
    107, 113
Carroll, Lewis, 108
Cassirer, Ernst, 108
Chadwick, Henry, 118
Christian fantasy, 18